UNBEATABLE

UNBEATABLE

The Story of the 2018 West Allegheny
High School Boys' Soccer
State Championship

BRENT DRAGISICH

To order additional copies of this book, contact:
Xlibris
1-888-795-4274
www.Xlibris.com
Orders@Xlibris.com
795069

The book *Unbeatable* is dedicated to all the West Allegheny soccer parents, friends, siblings, alumni, supporters, coaches, administration, and the wonderful people in the West Allegheny community that have cheered for us and helped us along the way. The ten thousand hours of work that the boys put into their soccer careers have led them to this monumental success. Because of this hard work, they are now etched forever in West Allegheny soccer history. It takes a village to raise boys and turn them into men, and we certainly had the support of the entire village along the way!

CONTENTS

Introduction ix

Chapter 1 How Did It Start? 1
Chapter 2 Keep Them Playing Together! 10
Chapter 3 The Middle School Years 15
Chapter 4 M7 Early High School Years 18
Chapter 5 Some Injuries Along the Way 21
Chapter 6 Sophomore/Junior Season and the Comeback 25
Chapter 7 Highmark and 2017 PIAA Playoffs 33
Chapter 8 M7 Senior Season Begins 38
Chapter 9 2018 Playoff Run Begins 49
Chapter 10 Stress = WPIAL Semifinal Games! 52
Chapter 11 The Road to Hershey! 65
Chapter 12 Enter Gabe Haines! 71
Chapter 13 Hershey Bound! 80
Chapter 14 The Final Game 85
Chapter 15 A Community Rallies 94
Chapter 16 National Spotlight and Individual Honors 96
Chapter 17 Where Did Unbeatable Come From? 98
Chapter 18 2013 vs. 2018 101
Chapter 19 Honoring West A and M7 108
Chapter 20 Memories and Parent Messages 113
Chapter 21 Quotes from Our Team 127

INTRODUCTION

If you have competed in high school sports, you know how hard it is to win a state championship. Pennsylvania is a big state, with great competition in all sports. There are programs with deep traditions and winning cultures. A lot of factors go into winning a state championship: developing youth players, having a core group of players that have soccer as their primary sport, and cultivating an environment that breeds competition. You need coaches that have the knowledge and skill to put players in the right positions to get the most out of them. You have to deal with injuries during the course of a season that consists of twenty-five games over a three-month period of time.

It can be a daunting task. But if you succeed, the rewards can last a lifetime. The memories you created along the way will last a lifetime. Sports has a way of doing that. It can cause the shyest of kids to show excitement. It can teach the most confident kids lessons in humility. Soccer is a game where a team of individuals can come together and put individual achievement aside for the greater good of the team.

The 2018 soccer season at West Allegheny High School did just that for the soccer players and the families that supported them through the years. When each season starts, it's a blank slate that begins with a 0-0 record. What are sometimes forgotten with each new season are the years of sacrifice, work, and tribulations that brought you here. What is important is that you remember those bonds with teammates. You remember the friendships with other families that lived the stressful games and moments with you. You remember the sacrifices of weekends away from home while at soccer tournaments. You remember the hours of practice in the heat, cold, rain, snow, and sleet.

My name is Brent Dragisich. I am a soccer dad with three kids, Nathan, Johnny, and Tiffany. My son, Nathan, is a senior on the team, and my son Johnny is a freshman on the team. I coached many of the boys on this team at the youth level, through indoor soccer and recreational leagues, and I've watched them grow into fine young men. I never imagined I would become a soccer dad, as I never played a day of competitive soccer in my life. I think the story of this team is a unique, fun, positive, and an interesting story. It has its moments of pure joy and some moments of heartache.

Unbeatable is written from my perspective of the unsuspecting journey I witnessed over the last fourteen years of watching, coaching, and cheering for these boys. *Unbeatable* is the story of the 2018 West Allegheny boys' soccer team and will take a close look at the journey of the players, coaches, families, games, moments, and memories that culminated in the first Pennsylvania state championship in West Allegheny Soccer history.

CHAPTER 1

How Did It Start?

How did the West Allegheny High School 2018 soccer team come together? What made them put all the years of practice, miles of travel, and hard work into soccer? Why did they want this state championship so much? This team was years in the making. Many of these boys started playing together in first grade, some even earlier. The West Allegheny 2018 soccer team is a special group indeed. The West Allegheny 2018 senior class has a very special bond. And this bond led this team to a tremendous legacy at West Allegheny High School.

Who are these West Allegheny soccer seniors? They are the graduating class of 2019. They are Nathan Dragisich, Evan Blunkosky, Braden Wurst, Justin Shaytar, Gabe Haines, Benny Farelli, and Antonio Fiordilino. I refer to this group of seven seniors as the *Magnificent Seven*, or *M7*. This is a group that has a bond and a friendship that is incredibly special. They have been through everything together. They are friends and schoolmates. Some live on the same street and in the same neighborhood. They have played multiple sports together over the years: baseball, basketball, and played hours of backyard sports together. They have grown up together, supported each other, shared secrets with each other, and have hours of shared laughter together. They are more than just friends; they have become brothers.

Let's meet this group of seniors we know as the Magnificent Seven and tell you about the senior group that would lead our team in 2018.

Evan Blunkosky, captain. As a respected leader on the team, Evan is a polite young man that can turn the switch and be a force with an aggressive style of play on the field. He's a tall and lean multisport player. He excelled at basketball in high school and also played baseball in his early days. He stands at 6'2" and 160 pounds with a great hairdo at all times! Evan plays the wing position and always has a fearless style on header balls.

Nathan Dragisich, two-year captain. Nate is a shy young man off the field but a silent assassin on the field, an intensely competitive player on the field but doesn't like the spotlight off the field. Two very different people emerge on and off the soccer field. Standing at 5'8" and 145 pounds, he was never the biggest kid on the field. But he is highly skilled, a great scorer, and very unselfish. Nate hates losing more than he loves winning.

Braden Wurst, captain, was the team's rock in the net and the leader of the defense. He grew up on soccer fields with his older brother Collin. He is a vocal leader on the team. Standing at 5'9" and 155 pounds, Braden is a highly athletic young man, and was one of the top goalies in the WPIAL all four years of his West Allegheny career. Braden was easily spotted all season in his bright orange goal keeper kit.

Benny Farelli is a highly skilled and very quick player with great footwork. Like many of our boys, he is a quiet, soft-spoken, and polite young man that is highly competitive. He is very well liked by his teammates and is a friend to all. Standing at 5'10" and a solid 150 pounds, Benny stands out with a great head of curly hair. He has a lot of finesse in his style of play. He is a hard worker and a very versatile player.

Gabe Haines is an outgoing young man that is full of style. He also has perfect hair, earrings, and is a sharp-dressed man. His great sense of humor keeps the team laughing. With a big body at 6'2" and 170 pounds and he's a versatile player that has held multiple positions over the years. Gabe is highly skilled, with great foot work and dribbling skills.

Justin Shaytar is a classic blue-collar player, a true workhorse. He's a quiet and shy young man who is known for his intelligence on the field and in the classroom. Though quiet, he is very easy to talk to. Standing at 5'7" and a strong 150-pound frame, Justin is a consummate worker and always hustles. He is highly coachable, and he listens to everything you say. He hustles, works hard, never complains, never argues. He is humble in victory, and classy in defeat.

Antonio Fiordilino can always be counted on for a laugh. He's very well liked by his teammates. He's a tall and slender young man, standing at 6'4", 145 pounds, with jet-black hair pulled back in a headband. Tony is a skilled player and a hard worker with a scrappy soccer style.

Now that we have met our M7 boys, let's talk about the families that make up the M7. What is interesting is that only one of the M7 families actually grew up in the West Allegheny school district. Brent and Malinda Dragisich both grew up in Weirton, West Virginia. Doug Wurst grew up in Dayton, Ohio, while Erin Wurst grew up in the Beaver, PA area. Doug and Erin met at Bowling Green University. The Fiordilinos, Mario and Debi, both have Michigan roots and grew up in the suburbs of Detroit. Kris Blunkosky grew up in neighboring South Fayette, while Kim Blunkosky went to Cornell HS in the Pittsburgh area. Dave Haines grew up two hours northeast of Pittsburgh in Brookville, Pennsylvania, while Kristin Haines went to Thomas Jefferson HS. Jeff Farelli graduated from Center High School while Louise Farelli graduated from Fort Cherry HS. John and Marice Shaytar were West Allegheny HS graduates. But they are the only ones!

Thinking about the life events that brought this group of players together fascinates me. What if some of these boys ended up at neighboring school districts? What if Kris and Kim Blunkosky decided to live in the neighboring South Fayette school district where Kris grew up? Evan could have been a member of our rival, South Fayette HS. What if Dave and Kristin Haines decided to move to the Thomas Jefferson school district? Gabe Haines could be wearing a Thomas Jefferson uniform. When Malinda and I bought our first house, we lived in the Chartiers Valley School District. We chose to move to West Allegheny when Nate was three years old since it was closer to grandparents that lived in Weirton. What if we decided to stay in the CV school district? We didn't move here for soccer. The same with the Wurst and Fiordilino families. Because of jobs and careers, they made West Allegheny the place they would raise their families, and thank goodness they did!

Our own coach of West Allegheny soccer, Kevin Amos, is a Mt. Lebanon HS graduate, and his wife Kathy Amos went to Moon Area HS. Kevin and Kathy Amos have six children, two of whom, Fletcher and Keegan, are on the 2018 team. What if they wanted to live within one of the districts where they grew up? How would things be different? The old cliché that "things happen for a reason" is true for the M7 and families. I imagine if you ask, each family can list several reasons that could have led them to live in another school district. Everyone had choices, but what made us all choose West Allegheny?

West Allegheny High School is twenty miles due west of downtown Pittsburgh, and a short 10 to 15-minute drive to the Pittsburgh International Airport. It's nestled in the farmlands of

Western, Pennsylvania with a blue-collar attitude. West Allegheny is a community made up of North Fayette, Oakdale, and Findlay townships and is one of the largest school districts in Allegheny County from a geographical standpoint. A lot of undeveloped land still exists for more housing and business development over the next several decades.

Over the past twenty years, farms and wooded areas have turned into housing developments. Homes were being built in the area due to the large investment in the nearby airport, and the cost of living in Pittsburgh has always been considered to be affordable. The area was growing; a lot of younger families were buying houses to raise their families. This drew a lot of our families to the West Allegheny school district.

Back in 2005, the earliest meeting of the first two M7 players came together at the Montour Run YMCA. Senior captains and best friends, Nathan Dragisich and Evan Blunkosky met each other at the age of four for the first time. Their friendship and soccer skills have gotten stronger every year since. Watching them grow up and seeing their successes, along with developing a close friendship has been extra special.

When Nate was four, my wife, Malinda, and I discussed enrolling Nate in activities where he could interact with other kids. I grew up playing basketball and running track with zero soccer experience. Basketball seemed too early for Nate at the age of four, while baseball or T-ball seemed like a lot of standing around.

Playing soccer, Nate could run around and have some fun. With him being my oldest, I was eager to be involved, even though I knew nothing about soccer. On we went to the local YMCA and signed Nathan up for a session of soccer, and I volunteered to be the coach.

As my team showed up on the first day, I checked off the players' names. One was Evan Blunkosky. He was similar to Nate, with a shy demeanor. He and Nate seemed to hit it off right away, and they ran around together during practices. I tried to make the practices and games fun, make the kids laugh, run around, and not take anything too seriously-they were four! Mission accomplished, as Nate wanted to keep playing.

My first love growing up was basketball, and I ended up going to college on a track and cross-country scholarship. Initially, I tried to steer Nate toward basketball at a young age. We had Nerf hoops before we ever owned a soccer ball. I even installed a basketball court in our backyard when Nathan was five and Johnny was two years old. Looking back, I wish I had planted grass and put up two soccer nets. But we did get a lot of use out of our concrete soccer field!

About six months after Nathan and Evan met at the YMCA, we were walking in my neighborhood with Nathan and a car drove past. I made eye contact with the driver. She looked familiar. As they pulled into their driveway, I realized it was Evan's mom, Kim Blunkosky. Evan got out of the car and, in a shy voice, said, "Hi Coach Brent." Evan and Nate were happy to see one another. I was happy to know a boy Nate's age in our neighborhood. They have remained best friends to this day. They have spent countless hours together in the neighborhood playing backyard soccer, basketball, and other sports. They and other team members and neighborhood kids have had many sleepovers, evenings building bonfires, and running around together. But we can always say that Nate and Evan played their first ever soccer game together at the YMCA-very special!

Another player on that first YMCA team was another neighborhood boy, Jimmy Ervin. Jimmy didn't continue his soccer career. But Jimmy's younger brother Jaxon plays, as does and our younger son Johnny. Both boys were freshmen during the 2018 season and had a big impact on the state championship team. Both also ran around the YMCA in diapers that year I coached Evan, Nathan, and Jimmy. Jimmy is also best friends with Nate and Evan. They are a very close group!

We also met Benny Farelli and his family through the YMCA. Benny was never on Nate's team at the YMCA, but they played each session, and we saw the Farelli family often over our time at the YMCA. Benny was always a skilled player with solid footwork and speed. We were happily surprised to see Benny at our first WAYSA soccer session, as we did not know he was from the WA school district.

During our first few years of living in the West Allegheny area, and after playing soccer at the YMCA, we met Coach Kevin Amos and his family when they moved into the neighborhood in 2005. At the time, Kevin Amos was running WAYSA (West Allegheny Youth Soccer Association) and had recently started coaching the West Allegheny High School team. His oldest sons, Tyler and Kasey, played for the high school team. Kevin told us about the WAYSA program. His other children included Cooper, Tatum, Fletcher, and Keegan. Fletcher and Keegan are similar in age to Nathan and Johnny.

We were excited to register Nathan for the WAYSA community league. Nate loved playing soccer. Even at a young age, Nate seemed to excel at soccer. I still believed he would play basketball someday (boy, was I wrong), but soccer would at least be a great way for him to make friends. WAYSA is where so much began.

There are many people that have played a part in building this 2018 West Allegheny state championship team, especially in the years leading up to 2018. First, you have Coach Kevin Amos, along with assistant coaches Derek McCracken and Johnny Aromando, who were instrumental in taking over WAYSA and developing players at the younger ages. Derek had two boys that played big roles in West Allegheny's early soccer success. All of Kevin's boys played West Allegheny soccer. His son Fletcher would become a key member of the 2018 team. Johnny Aromando had two sons, Danny and Christian, that both played soccer and had success as West Allegheny soccer players a few years before the M7.

Another key person in this story is Doug Wurst. I continued to coach at WAYSA. I enjoyed volunteering to coach the kids and make it fun for them. At one of the Saturday morning games at the Youthtowne Soccer facility, after we played a 4 vs. 4 game, a gentleman came over to me and introduced himself. It was Doug Wurst. His son Braden, our future GK and four-year varsity starter, was Nate's age and played on a different team at WAYSA.

Doug and I spoke about moving to the area, where we lived, and some general small talk. Doug had an older son that was four years older than Braden, and a daughter, Megan. Doug's older son, Collin, was an avid soccer player. Doug was a soccer guy; his sons loved soccer, so it seemed that Braden was in it for the long haul. Doug and I hit it off right away. We would always speak about the program, Collin, and our boys during Saturdays at WAYSA.

The next member of M7 that I met was Gabe Haines. What first caught my attention was Gabe's long, flowing hair on the WAYSA field. He had the best hair I had ever seen on a five-year-old. Over the years, the cool hair evolved. He also wore Rec Specs early on, which made him look even cooler. Gabe became an important part of our state championship team… and supplied an unforgettable memory.

I met the next member of M7 during the first day of preschool at St. Columbkille Church. The first day of preschool for Nate was stressful. Nate was a shy boy, and it was hard taking him to a new place without him screaming for us not to leave him. He was a clinger! This is when I met the Shaytar twins, Justin and Stacia, on the first day of preschool. Justin's mom, Marice Shaytar, was one of the nicest people you will ever meet. And since she was from West Allegheny, she knew a lot about the area and the school district. When we found out that they lived right down the road from us, it was instant friendship! Justin and Nate got along great; they were both into sports, so they had many playdates when they were young.

The final member of the M7 that I met was Antonio Fiordilino. I first met Tony on a baseball field. I also coached Nate's first tee-ball team, and Antonio was on the team. I have a funny but embarrassing first memory of meeting Antonio. Debi Fiordilino brought over Antonio to our first baseball practice. Antonio came a little late to the practice, and we were doing some drills. Antonio, a skinny kid who had a big smile on his face, was filled with energy. I told him to get in line as we were practicing throwing and catching.

As Antonio took his first turn, I threw the ball about ten feet in the air. Antonio held his glove out, ready to make the catch. The ball completely missed his glove and smacked him in the nose. I looked at him and he looked at me with a stunned look, and I thought, *Oh crap, is he going to cry?* He held it in for a few seconds, but then the tears came. Debi walked over as if to say, "He's been here for three minutes, and you already hit him in the face with the ball?"

I remember feeling awful about it, but he quickly recovered, and Debi and I laughed about it. That was my first meeting with Antonio! On the soccer field, Antonio was a player that made tremendous improvement over his soccer career at West Allegheny. In the beginning, he was a skinny and a fairly uncoordinated player. But he was a hard worker, he had fun doing it, and every year, he got better and better. He was a huge part of our success in 2018 and scored some very big goals along the way. Antonio also lives in the same neighborhood as Nate and Evan. Nate, Evan, Antonio, and Jimmy are the four musketeers. Always together!

So, we have now met the Magnificent 7: Nate, Evan, Benny, Braden, Gabe, Justin, and Antonio. Over the years, other players have come and gone from the team. Kids ended up excelling at other sports, or eventually just decided not to play soccer, great kids like Johnny Walls, Benny Schaupp, Clayton Rupnik, Logan Malatak, Jake Costantino, John Rink, Alex Berhosky, and Logan Scheider. They all played great roles over the years either through our indoor soccer days, our Cup soccer days with STM, and our WAYSA travel soccer days.

CHAPTER 2

Keep Them Playing Together!

West Allegheny also had a group of kids a school year younger than our Magnificent Seven that became vital to our success. Fletcher Amos, Caleb Miller, and Gavin Chappel were all soccer kids from soccer families and in the 2020 graduating class. Gavin's dad, Scott, played for West Allegheny soccer in the 1990's. Scott's team won the first section championship in West Allegheny history. Gavin's mom, Heather, has been highly involved in the WAYSA organization and is a board member on the West A Soccer Boosters. The Chappel's are a great soccer family!

Fletcher Amos has soccer in his blood. His dad is West A soccer Head Coach Kevin Amos. Fletcher's three older brothers all played soccer for West A. Kevin Amos also played D1 soccer at Robert Morris University. West A soccer and the Amos family go hand and hand.

Caleb Miller was a great player at an early age. Soccer was his passion and he has always played at a high level. Caleb has always been a defender, and he is a great defender. He has a strong left foot and a high soccer IQ. Caleb's mom, Sandi, is a schoolteacher and our team photographer. She is the owner of Blink of an Eye Photography. Sandi has captured so many special memories in photos. West A is so grateful for having Sandi on the sidelines taking these incredible pictures, which are used throughout this book. So, between our Magnificent Seven, along with Fletcher, Caleb, and Gavin a year behind, a great foundation for success was being laid.

I said it already, but Doug Wurst deserves a lot of credit for building this foundation, and here is why. Doug was highly involved with his oldest son, Collin, in West Allegheny Soccer. Doug coached Collins group of boys during their youth years. This group set the bar high and gave West Allegheny its first WPIAL championship and its first appearance in the state finals in 2013. That state final ended in a heartbreaking 1-0 loss. But what a group of players they had during those years: Collin Wurst, Zach Graziani, Cooper Amos, Mike Cummings, Kyle McCracken, Pat Harmon, Josh Kolarac, and Spencer Wolfe, to name a few. They laid a great foundation of success for the West Allegheny program, and Doug Wurst was their coach through those years.

I borrowed Doug's model when our current freshman boys were in first grade. I began to assemble a team with my son Johnny Dragisich. Tracy Pustover and I would coach a group that included, Jaxon Ervin, Keegan Amos, Will Douglas, Joseph Pustover, Mason Day, Trevor Day, Christian Brady, and Tyler Rosborough. Of this group, Jaxon Ervin started every varsity game as a freshman. Will Douglas and Johnny Dragisich earned substantial varsity playing time and Will started several games as a freshman. Johnny and Joseph each started one game during their freshman season. Keegan

Amos, Mason Day, and Trevor Day each earned some varsity playing time as well. Our young freshmen in the class of 2022 will be a force!

Years ago, nearing the end of a WAYSA fall season, Doug Wurst and I were talking, and he said, "Your son is a pretty good player. Would you have an interest in him playing indoor soccer?" I honestly didn't even know there were indoor soccer leagues for kids this young. Doug mentioned that a soccer parent named Ron Graziani, who has a son a year older than the M7 group, was coaching a team that played at the Pittsburgh Sportrak in Sewickley. Well, OK, we were in!

Ron Graziani also had a son named Nate. The team during the first year of indoor soccer was of kids ages kindergarten to second grade. The indoor games were competitive, but it was like herding cats at times. Ron Graziani was a great coach. He was patient, kind, caring, and he always promoted hard work and good sportsmanship. Our practices for indoor soccer would be held at the old West Allegheny library gym on Old Steubenville Pike.

The library gym was a tile floor basketball court connected to the West Allegheny public library. It was an old, concrete-block building that was somewhat rundown and outdated. The gym was quite small with a musty smell to it. It was by no means a soccer paradise, but it was a great place to train a group of first graders who didn't know the difference anyway! I always enjoyed Ron Graziani working with the boys and doing fun drills. The Numbers Game was especially fun and brought out the fun and competitiveness in the boys. I'm sure each boy has fond memories of the Numbers Game and practicing at the old library gym.

Ron taught the boys the basics, a good first touch, how to stay in your position and not do the beehive of just running after the ball all game. Each player was getting to play every position on the field. Learning each position was very important. Each child played the goalie position. It was fun watching them develop and learn the game.

The following year, as the number of players in West Allegheny soccer continued to grow, we made the decision to make a team based on school year. Our M7 boys were in the second grade when the decision was made to put our M7 players together for indoor soccer. Doug and I coached them. Ron Graziani and Michelle Abbott coached the boys that were a school year older and part of the 2018 graduating class.

When the boys were eight years old, Doug talked about getting a group of boys to play Cup soccer. My first question was, "What is Cup soccer?" That is how little I knew about soccer. After Doug filled me in, we got our M7 boys to play with a cup team named the Steel Town Magic, or STM. Our M7, along with Fletcher Amos and a few others, learned under Coach Adam Hunter of STM.

It was great to have them play better competition in the Pittsburgh area, travel to tournaments in surrounding states, and get coached by a non-West Allegheny parent. Over the years, different boys moved on to different Cup teams. Nate joined the Pittsburgh Riverhounds Academy. Gabe Haines went to Century United and Beadling, and ended up with the Pittsburgh Riverhounds. Benny, Justin, and Evan all played for FC Pittsburgh. Braden played for Century United. Fletcher Amos played for years with Beadling until moving to the Pittsburgh Riverhounds during his sophomore year of high school.

These boys loved the game and played year-round. Despite being on different club teams, we still had them playing together as a West A team during the fall and spring WAYSA travel seasons, and during the winter indoor leagues. Thank you, Doug Wurst, for showing us the way and keeping the boys together!

During these winter indoor sessions, we even developed some early rivalries. We always had some great games against teams from Mt. Lebanon, South Fayette, and Peters Township. The M7 boys played the older team from West A that Ron Graziani coached, which was always a fun rivalry. But the boys took it *very* seriously. This was their personal Super Bowl. The boys always looked forward to the West A vs. West A matchup. And both sides can say they won a few of those highly intense games.

Over the years, we would also do some 3 vs. 3 tournaments in the Pittsburgh area, some futsal tournaments, and many holiday indoor tournaments. The boys were having fun. They loved playing together. They were developing great friendships, and we were also experiencing some success.

CHAPTER 3

The Middle School Years

When the M7 moved into middle school, there was a solid group of players on the team. West Allegheny Middle School soccer was coached by Tom Jackson and Elliot Constantine, and it included seventh and eighth graders. Elliot was a former player at Robert Morris University and is a close friend of Kevin Amos and Johnny Aramondo. Tom Jackson has sons that have played in the West A program in years past. Our eighth graders were a solid group that included Nate Graziani, Steven Abbott, Jake Schiefelbein, Mike Bagnell, JD Eger, Zach Porter, and Daniel Tome, to name several.

This is the group that learned under Ron Graziani, so they had a great soccer foundation. Our M7 group was now in seventh grade.

Though we had talent on the team, we didn't necessarily have huge success, but we were improving. During the 2013 middle school season, we finished with a respectable 7-4-2 record. Our losses were to Quaker Valley, South Fayette, Montour, and Ambridge. Several of those teams would be high school section opponents in a few years. At that point, not many people looked at our team with high hopes of a future state championship.

Middle school soccer at West A is intentionally structured to develop players. We didn't always have the strongest eleven players on the field. Coaches Jackson and Constantine had twenty-five players on the roster, and all the players received some level of playing time. West A wanted to be competitive but also give every player the opportunity to improve. We were competing, winning some, losing some, and staying competitive. But during this season, one game really stood out that I use as an example of our upcoming improvement as a team.

In early October of 2013, we played Ambridge on our home field at McKee Elementary. We were pounded by Ambridge Middle School 8-0 in an overwhelming loss. We were completely dominated. They had our boys frustrated, overwhelmed, and the boys left with their heads hanging and some in tears. It was one of the worst beatings I had ever seen our boys take.

As I walked away from the field, I overheard two parents from Ambridge. They talked about how in 3 or 4 years when this group of Ambridge players got to high school, they would be very hard to beat and "it could be a team that wins some WPIAL and state titles." This was a team expected to dominate for Ambridge.

As I listened to their conversation, I couldn't disagree. They had a solid team and just overpowered us. I tell that story as a reminder of what can change over the years. During the M7 junior and senior years, which equates to the same players involved in the seventh and eighth grade middle school team, we had a record of 4-0 vs.

Ambridge over two seasons. The combined score was 16-0 in those four games. Ambridge did make the WPIAL playoffs both seasons, but they had early departures in the playoffs.

What was the catalyst for change in these teams? When did the change in the teams take effect? Ambridge still had some very good players. But our West A program was doing a great job of developing our boys. Additionally, the dedication including additional training with their respective cup teams really paid dividends for our group.

Our other losses during that middle school season were to South Fayette (5-0), Quaker Valley (5-0), and Montour (5-2). During the M7 junior and senior seasons, we had a 3-0 record vs. South Fayette. We beat Quaker Valley 4-2 during the M7 senior season. We had a 4-1 record vs. Montour over the junior and senior M7 seasons. In three years' time, the boys went from a good middle school team to a high school team that consistently dominated its section.

During the eighth grade season for M7, combined with seventh graders Fletcher Amos, Gavin Chappel, and Caleb Miller, we had a strong 10-1-1 season. We had wins over South Fayette, Ambridge, and Quaker Valley, all of whom beat us the previous season. The eighth grade season is really when you could see the tide was starting to turn.

Our boys were maturing, developing their skills, and improving in every aspect of soccer. We also had many players that were playing Cup soccer year-round. They were getting touches on the ball, playing against great competition and enjoying the game. And they were all close friends! It was still way too early to think that a state championship awaited us. But when Doug Wurst and I spoke, we both felt the future looked bright!

CHAPTER 4

M7 Early High School Years

As our M7 group reached their freshman year of high school, West Allegheny had just completed two of the most successful seasons in program history during 2013 and 2014. A WPIAL championship and a state championship appearance were achieved. Several players were also moving on to college programs and playing at the next level.

The West A state championship appearance in the 2013 season ended in a heartbreaking 1-0 OT loss to Holy Ghost Prep. Our coaches and alumni still talk about that game as it ended with a controversial non-call after a Holy Ghost player knocked down the West Allegheny goalkeeper, Spencer Wolfe, which led to the game-winning goal in OT. You certainly remember the tough losses as much as you remember the great wins. Anger still exists in the 2013 teams' voices when talking about the Holy Ghost Prep state championship game.

The players on the West Allegheny teams during these two great seasons in 2013 and 2014 were some of the best to ever come out of West Allegheny. Zach Graziani, Ron's middle son, was a shut-down center back, and a high school All-American who went on to play D1 soccer at Robert Morris University. Collin Wurst ended his high school career as the third all-time leading scorer in West A history and went on to play at St. Francis University. Mike Cummings was the second all-time leading scorer in West A history and headed to California University of PA to play soccer. Josh Kolarac was a tremendous left back during these two seasons and played four years at Penn State Behrend. Kyle McCracken also played at Penn State Behrend for a season in college. Cooper Amos was a sophomore and junior during those two seasons, and he finished his career as the all-time assists leader in West A history. He played one season at California University of PA.

The 2013 and 2014 West A soccer seasons were two of the most successful and dominant seasons in program history. This group compiled a two-season record of 39-6-4. Compare that with the 2017 and 2018 seasons, which was 43-5-1. Both groups had a tremendous stretch during those periods of time. The players from both teams debate which team was better, and what the outcome of a game between the two would be, which inspired chapter 18 – "2013 vs. 2018."

After these two great West A soccer seasons of 2013 and 2014, we certainly felt the loss of these great players following their departure. West Allegheny lacked depth of players in the incoming senior and junior class when the M7 were freshmen. We had a big-time talented player, Cooper Amos, who was our senior leader and leading scorer. We had some seniors that played soccer as a secondary sport, Ryan Cunningham and Jake Gazella-both great kids and athletes that had solid seasons. We had juniors Christian Aromando and Michael Starkman, and they were solid players on defense and well respected by their team. But the lack of depth in the upper classes left some opportunities for playing time with our young core group of freshmen.

Nathan Dragisich, Evan Blunkosky, and Braden Wurst immediately earned starting positions for the varsity team, coached by Kevin Amos. Benny Farelli and Justin Shaytar both saw some varsity playing time, and the boys learned a lot about the speed of the high school game. Antonio and Gabe both made the varsity roster and were prominent players on the junior varsity team. The M7 boys were fourteen years old playing against seventeen and eighteen-year-olds. I remember Nate Dragisich, a late bloomer, was 5'0" and 100 pounds his freshman season. He was very undersized compared to any junior or senior. Malinda and I just hoped and prayed he didn't get hurt!

The freshman season of M7 started out strong as we got off to a solid 6-1 start. Though the young boys took a beating, they did a lot of growing up during the early part of the season. However, our lack of depth and our inexperience eventually caught up with us during the season. M7's freshman season ended with a respectable 8-9-1 record, but we failed to qualify for the WPIAL playoffs. We limped into the final stretch of the season by losing six of our final seven games. Losses to South Fayette, Quaker Valley, Moon Area, Obama Academy, and Montour were the toughest ones to stomach. We still had a long way to go to become an elite WPIAL team, and the way the season ended showed how much work we still needed to do.

CHAPTER 5

Some Injuries Along the Way

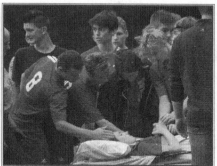

The four-year high school careers of M7 saw so many great moments. But along the way, we did see many challenges, setbacks, and injuries that come with high-level soccer. In all cases, we ended up coming back stronger from them. They're never easy to endure.

During Benny Farelli's junior year, he tore his ACL during a home game. An ACL injury involves a long recovery, intensive rehab, and ultimately leaves many questions regarding the long-term impact it can have on your game.

Benny worked extremely hard to come back from his ACL injury. When we had our epic comeback against South Fayette (which will be discussed in great detail), Benny was about three weeks post-surgery. When Evan Blunkosky put in the game winner, I saw our players who were sitting on the bench sprint across the field to join in the celebration. Benny Farelli did his best to join them, crutches and all, came across the field to celebrate the win with his team. My heart hurt for Benny as he was not able to be on the field. It's a testament to Benny that he was there with his team, and enjoying the moment.

Benny had a tremendous senior season after his ACL injury. Benny's best games were the final three games of the 2018 season.

Our games against Hershey, Franklin Regional, and Strath Haven in the PIAA playoffs were dominated by Benny at the holding mid position. He was flying around the field, making great decisions, and was truly a force. Sometimes when you don't score goals, it goes unnoticed. Benny Farelli was a big-time reason we beat Franklin Regional, as he completely shut down their forwards and attacking midfielders.

How good was Benny in the Franklin Regional state semifinal game? I honestly don't even remember the Franklin Regional forwards playing in the game, and one was an All-State selection, the other an All-WPIAL freshman. Benny, and our defense, dominated their forwards. Congratulations Benny for coming back strong, and having a huge impact after your injury.

In 2016, during the M7 sophomore year, we also went through a traumatic injury. Our junior captain, Nate Graziani, had an injury that anyone attending the game will not forget. Nate Graziani had a great career at West A. He comes from a great West A soccer family and is a solid all-around player.

On this day, we were playing a game against Sewickley Academy. Sewickley Academy is a small, private school but a perennial soccer powerhouse. With about four minutes left in the game, Nate Graz and a Sewickley player came together at full speed going after a ball. Their legs met, and boom, we heard and saw a leg go in a position that it should not go. It was evident right away that Nate Graz had suffered a broken leg. He lay on the ground, writhing in pain. Nate's parents, Ron and Kathy, who had attended *every* game during Nate's career, were not in attendance at this game. Looking back, I know they would have wanted to be there for Nate, but part of me is glad that they didn't witness this injury.

I remember running on to the field to help Nate and just try to calm him down and hold his hand. He was in a tremendous amount of pain. It's amazing to me how the body takes over though, and after a minute, Nate settled into what I would assume was a mild shock. We were very fortunate that day as a father of one of the Sewickley Academy players was an orthopedic surgeon. Dr. Mullholland took over Nate's care immediately on the field and actually set Nate's leg back in place. He also made a splint to secure Nate's leg. It was a godsend that he was there to help. Thank you, Dr. Mullholland.

As the ambulance arrived and we loaded Nate Graz in, I remember for the first time looking at the West A teammates that had just witnessed their leader go down with this horrific injury. What I saw was a team in utter mourning. There were a lot of tears and so much genuine concern. They all had a word of encouragement to Nate before he left. Michael Starkman, a great leader and a senior captain, said something to Nate that actually brought a smile to Nate's face. Soccer was secondary to what just happened. I saw a group of boys that were heartbroken over what just happened to their teammate. I am sure it's a memory that the boys will never forget.

As I drove away from the field, I called Ron Graziani on the phone. I wanted to tell him what great care Nate received and how tough Nate had been. I felt horrible for Ron and Kathy. I remember hanging up the phone after speaking to Ron for a few minutes, and emotions got the best of me, and I began to cry. My heart hurt for Nate and the Graziani family. It's never fun seeing something bad happen to a great kid and family.

But like Benny Farelli's junior season injury, this was Nate Graz's junior year. The same questions would be asked about how he would respond to coming back from that kind of injury. Well, Nate Graz had a tremendous senior season as our holding midfielder, and captain. He had an important pass in the South Fayette comeback game that led to the game equalizing goal (again, more details to come). Nate Graz went on to play D1 soccer at Robert Morris University. Though our state championship was a year after Nate left the program, he had a huge impact on West A soccer, as both a player and a leader.

The Graziani family is legendary in the history of West A soccer. Nate Graziani was a four-year starter. Zach Graziani was an All-American, a four-year starter, and one of the best center backs in West A history. Their oldest brother Tyler was a four-year starter and was the all-time leading goal scorer in West A history heading into the 2018 season. The Graziani family left a tremendous legacy of success at West Allegheny, both as athletes, as students, and as great people.

CHAPTER 6

Sophomore/Junior Season and the Comeback

The West Allegheny team of 2017, M7's junior season, caught a lot of people by surprise. We were coming off a decent 2016 season making the WPIAL playoffs as a thirteenth seed. The M7 group were sophomores during the 2016 season and were competitive throughout every game of the season. We had some solid wins, several ties, and most of our losses were by a one-goal differential.

In 2016, the team made the WPIAL playoffs as a thirteenth seed and opened some eyes with a first round upset of the fourth-ranked team, Belle Vernon, on their home turf. Goals from Steven Abbott, Nate Dragisich, and Evan Blunkosky sealed a 3-0 dominant win over a team that many thought had a chance to win the WPIAL.

In the 2016 WPIAL quarterfinals, we lost a hard-fought 1-0 game to eventual WPIAL champion, Chartiers Valley. It was a tight game, and we had several great opportunities to score. It was a game that we had a chance to win with a few solid scoring chances. But, instead, it ended our 2016 season. We played the last part of the 2016 season without one of our best players, Nate Graziani, who was recovering from his broken leg.

Our 2016 team finished with a below average 7-9-4 record. However, the West A faithful knew that this was a team in 2016 that started three freshmen and at times, five or six sophomores. Another year of experience for those players, along with bringing back a solid incoming senior class of Nate Graziani, Steven Abbott, and Jake Schiefelbein, among others, would be a great foundation for success in 2017.

Coach Amos talked a lot about how 2016 was a year that many of our games were one-goal losses, in addition to four ties. Doug Wurst and I talked about how these close games in 2016 would help us next season, and the boys would eventually learn how to win these close games. A year of physical and mental maturity and off-season practice would make us a force. How would this group perform in 2017?

The year 2017, the M7's junior season, did not disappoint! We lost our first game of the regular season 2-1 in OT in the Shaler HS Kickoff Tournament. Franklin Regional, a 4A school at the time, beat us on a questionable call that led to a PK in OT. But after that opening season loss, we ran the table with eighteen straight wins during the regular season. The boys beat section rival and a senior-laden Montour team twice during the regular season.

The second victory against Montour was on their home turf and clinched West A its first section title since 2014. The departure of the 2018 Montour senior class, and a shallow bench of upcoming players, would leave Montour at the bottom of the section just a year later. During the 2017 season, both West A victories over Montour in the regular season were comeback wins.

The first win against Montour was a great 2-1 comeback win at home. It was led by two Evan Blunkosky goals, which were both assisted by Nathan Dragisich. The goals were scored in a three-minute time span in front of a big and noisy West A crowd. The second regular season game over Montour was a 3-2 comeback victory that clinched our first section title since 2014. Goals from Nate Dragisich, Evan Blunkosky, and Gabe Haines allowed us to celebrate on Montour's home turf. It was a great team effort!

We finished the 2017 regular season as the #1 seed in the WPIAL with an 18-1 record. It was an amazing turnaround from our 7-9-4 record during the 2016 season. We entered the WPIAL playoffs playing very well and with a lot of confidence. Our first playoff game was against West Mifflin, and we breezed to a 9-0 win at West Allegheny Stadium.

Our second-round opponent was Belle Vernon, whom we had upset in the WPIAL playoffs during the 2016 season. This time, we were the higher seed and the game was played at Peters Township HS. Belle Vernon was a scary team. They had a big-time goal scorer, Markello Apodiakos. He was big, fast, strong, and a threat every time he touched the ball. Though the game had some back-and-forth moments, we did a great job containing Markello and ended up winning 4-1 with goals by Fletcher Amos, Gabe Haines, and two from Evan Blunkosky.

Now it was on to the 2017 WPIAL semifinals against our bitter rival, South Fayette. Make no mistake, we hate South Fayette. Yes, they have players that play cup soccer on the same team as some of our players, and off the field, we respect them and have developed friendships with them. But when West Allegheny and South Fayette meet on a soccer field, we hate each other, plain and simple. Earlier in the season, we beat South Fayette 2-1, but it was a game that we really dominated, so I felt confident that we could handle them again.

Well, South Fayette, to their credit, came to play. Despite us controlling possession for most of the game, we found ourselves down 2-0 late in the second half. It was a dreary, rainy, and cold day, with the game being played at a neutral site, North Allegheny HS. With only fifteen minutes left in the game, we had a two-goal deficit to overcome, and it looked very bleak.

South Fayette is a well-coached team. They did a great job of putting their best player on our top goal scorer, Nate Dragisich. We were not finding a lot of great opportunities. Things turned our way when senior Steven Abbott took a pass from Nate Dragisich and badly beat a South Fayette freshman defender for our first goal of the game with twelve minutes left in regulation. It was a great cutback move that froze the South Fayette defender-such an important goal by Steven Abbott. West Allegheny now had a pulse, and we were putting a ton of pressure on South Fayette. But would it be enough?

We continued to dominate South Fayette for the next seven minutes and put tons of pressure on their defense and goalie. With four minutes left in regulation, and still down 2-1, I remember Doug Wurst looking at me and saying, "We will get one more good scoring chance." He was right. With about one minute and thirty seconds left in the game, Evan Blunkosky played a long ball from deep in our defensive zone. The ball skipped under the foot of Fletcher Amos and onto the foot of Nate Dragisich, who was past midfield. Speedy senior, Steven Abbott, was flying down the right side of the field, and Nate played a perfect pass to Steven. In stride, Steven was behind the defense, one on one with the goalie, and shot the ball from fifteen yards out for what looked like the game tying goal. But the South Fayette goalie stuck his hand out and just got a piece of the shot. It was a great save, and the looks on our faces were of despair. We thought that our chance to tie was lost. I looked at Doug Wurst and said, "That might have been our chance."

I remember hearing the game announcer say, "One minute remaining in the game," over the loud speaker. Shortly after he said that, the ball was kicked towards the South Fayette goal, and safely into the arms of the South Fayette goalie. Our chances of winning seemed over. After an 18-1 regular season record and a #1 seed in the WPIAL, would we really be in the position to play a consolation game just to get into the state playoffs? The South Fayette goalie kicked the ball high into the air, and it bounced over midfield. We were now seventy-two yards away from the South Fayette goal with only forty seconds left in the game. Our chances were slim. Then, this happened.

Justin Shaytar, playing the right back position, did a great job of winning the ball over the South Fayette forward. Justin passed the ball ten yards up to Steven Abbott. Steven then one touched a pass ten yards back to Nate Graziani near mid-field. Nate Graziani kicked a left-footed pass twenty yards up the field to Nate Dragisich, who stood with his back facing the South Fayette goal. Nate took the pass at his chest area and toe-poked the ball behind him to Gavin Chappel. Gavin ran the ball down towards the left side of the field about twenty yards from the end line. Gavin looked up and saw Nate Dragisich sprinting down the middle of the field. Gavin slotted a perfect left-footed pass to Nate fifteen yards from the goal. Nate was now one on one with the South Fayette goalie. Running full speed, Nate quickly settled the ball and placed a right-footed shot past the outstretched hands of the goalie and into the lower right side of the goal. The game was now tied 2-2 with twenty-six seconds left in regulation!

The West A crowd was in absolutely chaos. We were screaming, yelling, high-fiving, hugging, and running around in utter disbelief. I remember running in the bleachers to hug Malinda and my family. I ran by my good friend and West A Soccer Booster president, Kristin Haines. Kristin had fractured her leg and was wearing a walking cast at the time. The cast was covered in a garbage bag to prevent it from getting wet on this rainy day. Kristin was in tears, crying with joy over what we just witnessed, with a soaking-wet walking cast. We still laugh about the wet walking cast today.

The video of the goal and the audio of the parents and West A supporters in the stands is both funny and amazing. On such a bad-weather day, it was mostly family and close friends in attendance. By the sound of the crowd, you would have thought that thousands of West A fans were in attendance. It was pure emotion and awesomeness. Complete chaos!!

The West A players and coaches were out of their minds as well. Evan Blunkosky was struggling towards the end of regulation with leg cramps. Once this goal was scored, it was almost like a bolt of energy went through him and our boys. Nathan Dragisich raised his arms as he sprinted to the corner and did a baseball slide near the far-corner flag. The rest of the team sprinted his way as Steven Abbott slid in to Nate. Fletcher Amos, after doing a front flip, slid in as well. Gavin Chappel, who was responsible for the great pass and assist, was as fired up as I have ever seen him. As he crossed midfield prior to the restart of play, he flexed his muscles, looked up at the sky, and let out a loud roar.

Evan Blunkosky, who was on the far side of the field, sprinted to the team celebration and grabbed Nate's jersey with both hands and was yelling something in Nates face. I'm still not sure what was said, but I'm sure it was awesome! I remember Nate Graziani hugging Nate and walking away and you could read his lips as he said, "Oh my God!" I also remember Justin Shaytar and Nate with a long hug after the rest of the team had started running back to the middle of the field. It was an amazing *team* goal. We were now heading into OT with *all* the momentum in our favor. I truly felt that it was just a matter of time.

On the other side, South Fayette was in complete agony after giving up this late goal. Their fans were quiet and in shock. On the game video, their players had their hands on their heads in complete disbelief. They yelled at each other, asking, "Who had him?" Someone missed an assignment and didn't mark-up Nate. Some of the South Fayette players raised their hand after the goal, hoping for an offsides call to bail them out. Not even close. Nate was five yards on side. South Fayette had victory in hand, and we really broke their hearts.

Their coaches were seen saying something to the referee as we set up for the restart. Not sure what they were questioning. They were grasping at straws. It was simply a great goal.

The first OT period saw a few decent opportunities from West A as we continued to control the ball, but the game remained tied. After the first OT period ended and the second OT period began, it started to set in that this game could go to PKs. With all the momentum we had coming into OT, I honestly did not want to give South Fayette a chance to win the game in PK's. Then, this happened.

With nine minutes left in the second OT period, Gavin Chappel attempted to cross a ball into the box. The ball deflected off of South Fayette out of bounds for a West Allegheny corner kick. Nate Dragisich lined up to take the corner. As Nate was preparing to take the corner kick, I noticed Evan Blunkosky continuing to stretch his legs as his leg cramps were once again bothering him. Our boys, and both teams, for that matter, were drained.

Nate played a ball into the center of the box, and it was headed into the air by a South Fayette player. Justin Shaytar, who won the ball to start the game-tying goal, once again made a great play to keep the ball alive, and he headed it back into the box. The ball landed near the foot of Evan Blunkosky about eleven yards from the goal. Evan turned and nailed a left-footed line drive that was headed right to the goalie. But this shot had some gas on it, and the field was wet, and the ball was wet.

The goalie was positioned perfectly to catch the ball. But, remember, wet field, wet ball, and a hard shot. The ball went right through the GK's arms and legs and settled into the back of the net for the game-winning golden goal! The boys in unison raised their arms in victory. Evan turned and ran towards our cheering section and ripped his jersey off as the leg cramps that bothered him were a distant memory. Evan leaped into the air and let out a loud *"Yes!"* as he pumped his first and punched the air. The West A bench cleared as the boys sprinted across the field. We were in celebration mode!

The team quickly mobbed Evan, as Fletcher Amos and Justin Shaytar got to him first. Soon the boys were standing on the side of the field in a large group, hugging and jumping up and down. It was funny to watch the replay of this as Gabe Haines struggled to get his rain-soaked Under Armour shirt off, and it briefly covered his face and head. Nathan Dragisich ran to the group celebration with his hands on his head, almost in disbelief with what just happened. It was amazing to watch this happiness and passion from the boys. We did it. We had completed a comeback of the ages, a comeback victory over our bitter and hated rival, South Fayette, 3-2.

Parents and West Allegheny fans were rain-soaked and exhausted, yet riding a wave of happiness and pride that is hard to explain. Parents hugged each other in the stands. There was disbelief as to what we just witnessed. After the postgame handshake with South Fayette, the boys made their way to the locker room to get changed. I wish we could have seen the scene in the locker room. But some things are meant to be with just the boys and the team.

The parents and fans walked to the back of the stadium to the locker room exit and greeted the boys as they boarded the team bus. We cheered, we chanted, "West A": we hugged, high-fived, and celebrated this moment that will live forever in West Allegheny soccer history. What a win! It was now on to Highmark Stadium to play Montour for a third time this season. We also guaranteed ourselves a spot in the PIAA state playoffs, as the top three teams in the WPIAL move on to the state tournament. This West A team was for real, and the cardiac kids just pulled off a comeback for the ages.

CHAPTER 7

Highmark and 2017 PIAA Playoffs

The 2017 season put West Allegheny on the map as a big-time contender in the WPIAL. With only three senior starters and eight sophomores and juniors in the starting line-up, there was no doubt that the future was bright. After our monumental comeback against South Fayette, we were now headed to Highmark Stadium for the WPIAL Championship game against Montour HS. Our two regular season games against Montour were tough battles. West Allegheny came out on top in both matches with one goal victories. Both games were evenly-matched with West Allegheny coming from behind to win in both games. This WPIAL championship would probably come down to the same kind of matchup. Montour was a senior-laden team with nine senior starters. With a lack of talent coming up in the younger ages, this was their year to get it done.

Highmark Stadium was buzzing with energy and emotion. It was a beautiful evening with cool temperatures in Pittsburgh-perfect soccer weather! A lot of students and fans from both sides had come to watch this highly anticipated matchup.

Our games with Montour are always physical and this game was no different. Both teams went back and forth with some good opportunities. The pace of the game was fast and intense. But a tough mistake led to a first-half goal for Montour, and we went into halftime down 1-0.

West Allegheny put a lot of pressure on Montour in the second half, but both teams were finding some good opportunities to score. With under five minutes left in the game, the score remained a 1-0 Montour lead, as we continued to apply some pressure and move some players forward. With four minutes left, West Allegheny had a tremendous scoring chance that made the crowd gasp.

As West Allegheny held possession in our offensive half, a ball was played into the box by Jake Schiefelbein. It was played from about thirty-five yards out and was a high floating ball and was starting its descent down about eight yards from the goal. The ball was perfectly headed by Nate Dragisich. The header had solid pace on it and looked as though the ball was going into the upper-right corner of the net. At the very last second, Montour senior goalkeeper, Brian Duggan, dove with his arm extended and just got a fingertip on the ball and deflected it over the net. It was an amazing save. The West Allegheny crowd was stunned and our players all had their hands on their head as we thought we had tied the game off of a great header. With only three minutes left, we were unable to repeat the magic of a late comeback that we had against South Fayette. The game ended with a 1-0 loss in the WPIAL championship. This game also ignited a social media feud with some of the departing Montour players that continues today.

After the game in a postgame interview, Coach Amos was talking about the boys recovering from this loss and getting ready for the PIAA playoffs. He made a comment that we will get the boys a hamburger, relax, and move on. The Montour players used the "burger" comment in social media to poke fun at our WPIAL loss to them. They posted a picture of their WPIAL championship rings and made reference to it: they made reference to it when we lost to Franklin Regional in the 2018 WPIAL championship. They ate their words (no pun intended) when we won the state championship, though! State championship burgers do taste good, Montour! The following season of 2018, we would beat Montour HS by a combined two-game score of 16-0. Needless to say, we no longer consider Montour a rival.

After the WPIAL championship loss to Montour, we now set off as the #2 seed from the WPIAL and began to prepare for our PIAA playoff run. Our first matchup was over two hours away in Clearfield, Pennsyvania, against Dubois HS. It would be interesting to see how the boys would respond. It was a frigid night in Clearfield PA. The boys came out strong and struck quickly and struck often. We responded with a convincing 7-0 win in a game that was never in doubt. A balanced scoring attack led our team as six players found the scoring column. Two goals by Evan Blunkosky and one goal each from Nate Dragisich, Nate Graziani, Fletcher Amos, Connor Blazer, and Jake Schiefelbein led the attack.

We were now headed to the quarter-final round of the PIAA playoffs. The game was being played in Altoona, Pennsylvania, at Mansion Park Field. Our quarter-final matchup was against Pennsylvania powerhouse Lower Dauphin High School. This was a scary team. They had three seniors that were headed to play soccer in college. Two were Division 1 players. One player, Jackson Becher, was the eventual PA State Soccer Player of the Year and was headed to Division 1, UMBC (University of Maryland Baltimore County). The defense was led by a Colgate University recruit, and they also had a player going to play at Slippery Rock University. Two of their junior starters were college-caliber players as well. They were a very good team. This would be a big test for us.

The West Allegheny boys came out strong and played a great first half. Despite Lower Dauphin seeing some good scoring chances, we held them scoreless in the first half. Braden made some key saves, and our defense was solid. In the first half, Caleb Miller had a beautiful set piece goal from twenty-five yards out to give us a 1-0 lead heading into halftime. Through forty minutes, the underdog West Allegheny Indians held a lead. But we knew the caliber of players and we witnessed some great play by Lower Dauphin in the first half, despite holding them scoreless.

Lower Dauphin came out with a lot of focus and pressure in the second half. They tied the game with thirty minutes left in the game off a goal by their leading scorer, Jason Becher. It was his 100th career high school goal. Only five minutes later they took a 2-1 lead. They were really putting pressure on us and the momentum of the game was starting to shift. They went up 3-1 at the eighteen-minute mark and things looked bleak for West Allegheny.

With fifteen minutes remaining in the game, a bad call that went against us might have put us back in the game. A foul was called on the Lower Dauphin goalie as he threw an intentional elbow at senior Steven Abbott after making a save near the edge of the goalie box. The foul was clearly committed inside the box and should have been a PK for West Allegheny. Remember, the goalie was holding the ball and never left the goalie box. The referee instead said the foul happened outside the box and gave us a set piece that we did not convert.

If we had a PK, maybe it turns into a different game. A PK makes it 3-2 and gives us some momentum and a chance has we headed into the final fifteen minutes of the game. The call did not go our way, and we were forced to take some chances late in the game, and we ended up losing the game 4-1. It was a disappointing end to our season. But Lower Dauphin was the better team on that day. There wasn't much we could say, and the kids knew it. After losing our first game of the season, and then winning nineteen games in a row, we finished the season by losing two of our last three games.

It was very sad to watch our 2017 seniors walking off the field for the last time with a loss. A lot of emotions come out in these young men. The underclassmen were saying goodbye to a great senior group that were both teammates and friends. They would no longer have the chance of playing on the same field together wearing a West Allegheny uniform. They had been on this journey together, and to have it end so suddenly hurts. Montour ended up losing to Lower Dauphin in the next round as well. Montour was down 3-0 at halftime, and they were never really in the game. West Allegheny at least gave Lower Dauphin a scare as we led 1-0 through the fifty-minute mark of the game.

Lower Dauphin would go on to win the state championship that year. I feel that the boys remembered the feeling of walking off the field with a loss. I remember the following year, Nate Dragisich was asked in an interview what his goal was for the 2018 season. His answer was, "I don't want to end the season with a loss." I think the 2017 Lower Dauphin and Montour loss really motivated this group of returning players to work hard in the off-season and make sure 2018 didn't end this way.

CHAPTER 8

M7 Senior Season Begins

The 2018 season brought a lot of excitement, along with high expectations. The 2017 season saw us win a section championship, finish with a WPIAL runner-up, and with an appearance in the PIAA quarterfinals. We were also returning our core group of starters that made a big impact in our successful 2017 campaign. Only three starters from the 2017 team graduated: Nate Graziani, Jake Schiefelbein, and Steven Abbott. All were very important parts of our 2017 success.

As parents, we felt that we had the players in place that could fill those spots, and we would put a very strong starting line-up on the field. Benny Farelli was recovered from his ACL injury that kept him out of the second half of the 2017 season. Connor Blazer was beginning his sophomore year after a solid freshman season where he earned a lot of varsity playing time. Senior Antonio Fiordilino was ready to step into a starting role. We also had a crop of solid freshman coming into the program. The 2018 season looked like it would have great competition for playing time, and our team depth was as good as I had ever seen.

The West Allegheny boys had a great off-season with their respective Cup teams as well. Nathan Dragisich had committed to play soccer at Duquesne University during his junior season. Several other seniors, Gabe Haines, Evan Blunkosky, Justin Shaytar, and Antonio Fiordilino were attending ID camps and getting college interest. During the summer, Nathan Dragisich was named a Club Soccer All-American with his Pittsburgh Riverhounds Academy team. The M7 boys were running the summer scrimmages and were showing great leadership to the underclassmen. They had a mentality that they wanted this to be a great season as they finished their West Allegheny soccer careers. They were in great condition as well. This group had worked *very* hard during the off-season.

The incoming freshman group, the class of 2022, was a big factor leading up to the season and a big question mark at the same time. This group had huge success in middle school soccer. During their eighth-grade season, they went undefeated while outscoring their opponents 97-0. Yes, that is not a typo. They did not give up a goal the entire season. The group was strong across the board. They were fierce competitors and we have a big freshman class with fourteen players. Yet, it is sometimes hard to judge how a freshman will handle playing against competition that is two and three years older. How many of our young players could make an impact and would they be ready for the challenge? That was a big question leading up to the season.

If you looked at our team coming into the start of the 2018 season, we had our M7 seniors that looked like they would all earn starting positions. Nathan, Evan, and Braden had started every game in their high school careers. Justin, Gabe, and Benny had started almost every game last year. Antonio received playing time at varsity and was continuing to develop into a very solid player. Our junior class, led by Fletcher Amos, Caleb Miller, and Gavin Chappel, started every varsity game in both the 2016 and 2017 seasons. It seemed fairly certain that our seven seniors and three juniors would be starters this year. So, there weren't a lot of open positions left in the starting line-up.

The freshman group in the class of 2022 was led by some highly talented players. Jaxon Ervin was a special talent that was skilled, fast, athletic, a great passer, and could score. Jaxon is the complete package. Will Douglas was a workhorse player that was aggressive, had a great non-stop motor, and great skill. Johnny Dragisich, Joseph Pustover, Mason Day, Keegan Amos, Logan Cunningham, Tyler Deramo, and several other players would all be vying for a varsity roster spot as well. Very simply, this group was special. Also, though our sophomore class was small with only three players, they were also very good. Connor Blazer received a lot of quality varsity time as a freshman, while Evan Kosenina and Ethan Taranto both contributed on the JV team. They all play cup soccer year-round and continue to develop. It was great to see this competitive atmosphere as the boys were all competing for playing time.

Each season, the boys officially kick off the new season with a five-day soccer camp. Soccer camp for the 2018 season had our boys and coaches heading to Slippery Rock University to have five days of practice, evaluation, team bonding, and conditioning. This is really where Coach Amos and his staff begin to piece the puzzle together. Roommates are assigned by coaches and they generally put an upper classman with an underclassman.

Camp is where our captains are voted on and announced. The 2018 season had four captains that would lead our team. Seniors Nathan Dragisich, Braden Wurst, Evan Blunkosky, and junior Fletcher Amos would be called upon to lead our team as captains this season. All four players had started every game of their high school careers. Nathan Dragisich had just received some pre-season exposure as he was put on the Top-Drawer Soccer High School All-American watch list, a great accomplishment because it names only 250 players in the country.

After a successful camp our team came back home and was ready to start the new school year at West Allegheny. We continued to train, practice, and work on our conditioning. The high school season is fast and busy with two or three games per week. Practice time can be scarce once the game season starts. Once school starts and we have a few practices, shortly after, we are ready for the regular season to start over the Labor Day weekend.

The 2018 season started off with a Labor Day weekend kickoff tournament at Plum High School. Plum HS was the host school and they are a 4A team. In WPIAL soccer, there are four divisions. Class 4A are the largest schools. West A is in class 3A. Fox Chapel, also a 4A school, and Gateway HS, a 3A school, were the other two teams in the tournament field. The competition was solid and the boys were itching to get on the field and compete. This Labor Day weekend was extremely hot with temperatures in the 90's. But the boys were eager to get the season started after two scrimmage games. One of our scrimmages was a 10-0 drubbing over OLSH. The other was a friendly scrimmage vs. Franklin Regional, who just this season had moved from the 4A Division to the 3A Division, where we compete. The scrimmage ended in a 1-1 tie. Hmmm, maybe we would see Franklin Regional later in the year-more to come on that!

Our first regular season game was against Gateway HS. We had never played Gateway HS in the four years that our senior class was in school. The West A boys came out with a bang as we showed our fire power in a convincing 8-0 win. As for our starting line-up, it was what a lot had expected it to be. We had our M7 seniors all earn starting spots, while juniors Gavin, Fletcher, and Caleb started as well. Finally, freshman Jaxon Ervin earned a starting role in the midfield position after a great camp and preseason. Two goals were scored by Nate and Fletcher, along with one each by Jaxon, Connor Blazer, Evan Blunkosky, and Johnny Dragisich. Sophomore Connor Blazer and freshman Johnny Dragisich saw a lot of playing time in the first game.

The championship game in the Plum tournament pitted us against Fox Chapel HS, who had beaten Plum HS the day before. Fox Chapel is always a great team in the 4A Division, and always has some solid players. We came out on top, 2-1 on goals by Fletcher Amos and freshman Will Douglas, who was another freshman seeing quality varsity playing time. A great start to the season, with two wins at the Plum HS tournament. We could also see that our team had a lot of depth. We didn't have to rely on just our starters this season. It was a solid 2-0 start to the young season.

Our first home game of the 2018 season had us taking on the Division 2A defending PIAA state champions, Quaker Valley HS. QV is a perennial soccer powerhouse. Their program has won multiple state championships, and year after year, they put great teams on the field. They are coached by Andrew Marshall, a former Pittsburgh Riverhounds professional team player. This would be a great non-section test early in the season for our boys. Remember, Quaker Valley is a team that beat us handily in the M7's middle school years.

And boy, did we make a statement! With four first-half goals, which included two by Connor Blazer, and one each by Nate Dragisich and Fletcher Amos, we sailed to a 4-1 halftime lead. We looked strong in what ended up a 4-2 win, with our boys really dominating possession and play. Quaker Valley would go on the play in both the WPIAL finals and they also made the PIAA state quarterfinals in 2018. This was a great barometer of where we stood early in the season. After this win over QV, we looked poised to have a very strong season and now stood at 3-0.

We followed our big victory over Quaker Valley with an easy 5-0 win over Beaver Area HS, which was our first section game of the year, to go 4-0 on the season. Our captains led the way in this one, with Nate Dragisich and Evan Blunkosky each scoring two, Fletcher Amos scoring one, while Braden Wurst and our defense put up a clean sheet. Early on in the season, we looked very focused and strong across the entire line-up. We were also getting strong contribution from our bench, as we were playing several subs during the game.

Next on the schedule was an important non-section game at home against South Fayette. South Fayette is a rivalry game, and always exciting for the boys. No pep talks needed in this one. They still hate us, and we still hate them. Remember the last time we were on the field with South Fayette? No doubt that both teams remember it well. We broke their hearts in our dramatic 3-2 WPIAL playoff comeback win of the ages, so revenge was no doubt on South Fayette's mind.

This game was getting some special attention, as Pittsburgh Soccer Now was covering the game. Pittsburgh Soccer Now is a local website committed to covering everything about soccer in the Pittsburgh area. The site was started by a passionate soccer guy named John Krysinski. John has done a fabulous job of making soccer an important sport in the Pittsburgh area. John covers the Pittsburgh Riverhounds professional team closely and has done great things covering college and high school soccer in the Pittsburgh area. John and his crew were doing a live radio broadcast of the game with postgame interviews. Matt Gajtka did the radio broadcast and cameraman, Ed Thompson, was also there to take action shots of the game. Thank you, John, for being such a great advocate of soccer in the Pittsburgh area. John is a genuinely nice guy.

Similar to last season's playoff victory, West Allegheny dominated possession and play over South Fayette, but we were not able to put a goal past the SF goalkeeper. We were clearly the better team, but a stingy defense by both teams kept the game scoreless well into the second half.

With about four minutes remaining in the game, we finally got a great scoring chance off a Benny Farelli crossing pass. Evan Blunkosky, who had briefly fallen down on the left side of the box, quickly jumped to his feet and took a loose ball and beat the goalie by placing a shot in the bottom left of the net. The boys all sprinted to the sideline on the spectator side of the field and, one by one, did a baseball slide on the wet field in celebration. The boys were pumped up, and we held on for a gutty 1-0 win over South Fayette. Another huge defensive effort by our stingy defense and another clean sheet by Braden Wurst. We would not see South Fayette again this season, as they were eliminated early in the 2018 WPIAL playoffs. With this big win over South Fayette, we moved to 5-0 on the season.

The next five games of the 2018 season were all section victories as we outscored and dominated our section opponents, 26-2. We had convincing victories over Moon, Obama, Montour, Blackhawk, and Ambridge over this stretch. A balanced scoring attack contributed to the wins as Nate Dragisich led the way with ten goals during the five-game stretch. Evan and Antonio each put in three, while Fletcher, Gabe, Jaxon, and Caleb all pitched in with two goals each. Our defense of Caleb Miller, Gavin Chappel, and Justin Shaytar, along with Braden Wurst in the net, were playing a dominant shutdown style.

During this five-game stretch we had an interesting 2-0 victory over Blackhawk. We saw our boys play down a man for the final fifty-five minutes of the game after a red card was issued to Fletcher Amos. It was a great team effort as the boys hunkered down and shut down a very good Blackhawk team. The red-card came with a 1-0 lead, so we really worked hard for this victory. Antonio Fiordilino drew a penalty in the box during the second half, and Nate was able to put the PK in for his second goal of the game, to give us a 2-0 lead. It was a great *team* victory! Benny Farelli was the man of the match as he really stepped up big in the holding midfield position to limit Blackhawk on the offensive end of the field.

Also, do you remember Ambridge, whom I mentioned during the middle school years when they beat us 8-0 during the M7's seventh grade season? We beat them 6-0 during this five-game stretch and completely dominated them. Seventh grade seemed so long ago.

We now stood at 10-0 for the season and we were ranked #1 in the WPIAL. Everyone was playing well and the boys remained focused. Our next five-game stretch saw even more domination from our boys. We outscored our next five opponents 30-1 to take us to 15-0 on the season. This included a 9-0 non-section win over Mount Lebanon, and four section wins over Beaver (4-0), Moon (2-1), Obama (8-0), and Montour (9-0). Yes, the Montour score was 9-0. I think they needed a burger, badly!

Once again, a balanced scoring attack was producing the offense during this 30-1 scoring margin. Nate Dragisich put in twelve goals, Jaxon Ervin had six, Fletcher Amos with five, Evan Blunkosky and Johnny Dragisich with two, and Gabe Haines with one. We also had first goals of the season from Mason Day and Eleon Wright. Eleon Wright, a senior, was a first-year player with West Allegheny. He moved to the area from Jamaica and lives in the school district with his uncle and aunt. He's a great young man that the boys really like, and he plans to join the Navy after high school graduation.

During this stretch, we had a tough match against a highly ranked Moon Area HS team. We had an interesting goal scored by Nate Dragisich during this game. Nate took a free kick from fifty-seven yards out. Nate blasted the ball high and long into the box. As the crowd of players was ten yards from the goal, the ball went over everyone, bounced between the crowd of players and the goalie, and went into the top of the net for a bizarre and unexpected goal. A great picture by Sandi Miller shows Nate shrugging his shoulders in an "I don't know" pose, wondering how the heck the ball went in the net. We were all surprised by this goal! But we ended up needing it as we went up 2-0 on two goals by Nate Dragisich, only to give one back late in the game. But we were able to hang on for a 2-1 win on the road at Moon.

During this five-game stretch, four more shutouts were added to the resume of Braden Wurst and our defense. The boys were playing great and stood at 15-0 with two more games on the regular season schedule. At this point, we also started paying attention to Nate Dragisich and his career goal and assist total. He was racking up some big numbers and came into the season needing thirty-two goals and fourteen assists to pass the all-time records for goals and assists in West Allegheny soccer history.

Through fifteen regular season games Nate had twenty-seven goals, twelve assists, and was closing in on both records. But, that was not the focus, and the records were not being talked about at all. The team goals were the central focus. Coming into the season though, those goal and assist records were held by two West A soccer greats, Tyler Graziani and Cooper Amos. Tyler ended his West Allegheny soccer career with seventy-three goals, while Cooper ended his career with forty-five assists.

Next up on the schedule was our second section game against Blackhawk. It was Senior Night, and we had a wonderful evening of celebrating our M7 seniors. The weather was perfect, the atmosphere was terrific, and we were confident that our great season would continue. Well, soccer can be a cruel sport sometimes!

Just when you think you are playing your best, sometimes things don't go your way. Soccer can be like that and this was one of those games. Blackhawk combined the efforts of their great goalie, Ethan Burawa, with an opportunistic goal late in the second-half off of a set piece to stun the undefeated Indians 1-0. It was a game where we had multiple chances early in the game and throughout the entire game to score and put away Blackhawk. But we just didn't convert, and it cost us the game. We dominated possession and chances, but just couldn't find the back of the net.

The boys walked off the field wondering what the heck went wrong. But, maybe this was a good wake-up call, a game that showed that we are not invincible. One of the West Allegheny Football coaches, Jimmy D'Amico, posted on Twitter some words of encouragement. He said, "In 2001, West A football lost to Blackhawk, on Senior Night, in a game we should have won. We ended up regrouping and winning the state championship that season." It was a nice pick-me-up and put things into perspective. We had one more game in the regular season, we had already won the section championship, and now it was time to regroup and get ready for the playoff run. Maybe this loss was a good thing in the long run.

The final game of the regular season was a solid 7-0 bounce-back win on the road over Ambridge. Our seniors led the way in our final regular season game as Nate had four goals, Benny had two, and Evan had one. During this game, Nathan Dragisich tallied two assists to become the all-time career assists leader for West Allegheny soccer, passing Cooper Amos for the all-time lead. Another shutout for Braden and our defense as well.

It was a game to regain our confidence and shake off our only loss of the year heading into the WPIAL playoffs. We finished the 2018 regular season with a 16-1 record, which would probably be good enough for a #1 or #2 seed in the WPIAL. Remember Franklin Regional, which we tied 1-1 in a pre-season scrimmage game? They finished their season undefeated with one tie, and a 17-0-1 record. I wonder if we will see them again. Or maybe even twice!

CHAPTER 9

2018 Playoff Run Begins

We headed into the 2018 WPIAL playoffs as a #2 seed as Franklin Regional was awarded the #1 seed. Our WPIAL playoff path would start with a home game against Greensburg Salem HS. We didn't know much about this team, but they had squeaked in as the #15 seed after placing fourth in their section. There were a few things to keep an eye on during this game.

Nathan Dragisich needed one goal to become the all-time leading goal scorer in West Allegheny soccer history. To make it even more special, the current goal leader, Tyler Graziani, was in attendance. A classy move by a classy individual to be there to witness his record possibly being broken. Well, it didn't take long as early in the first half, Nate took a shot that was stopped by the goalie. He then got his own rebound and put the first goal of the game in for a 1-0 lead. With the goal Nate became the all-time goal-scoring leader in West Allegheny soccer history.

It was a special moment as the team all celebrated the accomplishment with him. Duquesne University head soccer coach Chase Brooks happened to be in attendance to watch his recruit.

Nate's partner in crime, Evan Blunkosky, was the first to greet Nathan with a hug. An announcement was made over the PA system and the crowd acknowledged this great achievement with a loud ovation. I remember Nate coming to the midfield area, looking at the student section, and taking a bow. It was special to see Nate and the team enjoy this moment.

West Allegheny was far from being done scoring in this game though, as we dominated Greensburg Salem 13-0. Several West A players got in the scoring column, as Nate ended the game with four goals, Evan and Fletcher each had two, while Benny, Gabe, Antonio, Eleon, and Jaxon each put one in the net.

After the game, we did our man of the match interview with new scoring leader Nate Dragisich and alumni legend Tyler Graziani. Tyler is a 2012 graduate of West Allegheny and spoke glowingly about the team, the style in which they play the game, and how much he enjoyed watching them. When asked about his thoughts on our upcoming playoff journey, Tyler mentioned that there would be some bumps in the road along the way. If we could find a way to work through those bumps, he was confident we had a great chance to make a long run in the WPIAL and state playoffs. Bumps in the road? His words were really correct. As I look back, I say to Tyler Graziani, "Boy, were you right!"

Next up in the WPIAL playoffs was a quarterfinal match with Kiski Area HS. Kiski had a big win over Belle Vernon HS in the first round of the WPIAL playoffs. The past two years we had faced Belle Vernon in the WPIAL playoffs, and now we faced a new opponent that we had never played before and didn't know much about.

West Allegheny faced Kiski on a cold night at a neutral field, at Mars Area HS Field. Kiski brought a group of students that were really into the game and were making some noise. It was a very entertaining group of students that added a lot of fun to the game. It didn't take long to recognize that we were the better team. We really dominated possession the entire first half. However, we were not putting in some of our scoring chances. Nate had a PK that was saved, we hit a post, we had some shots go just wide, and others go high. We held a slim 1-0 lead at the end of the first half on a goal by Fletcher Amos.

However, the flood gates finally opened in the second half as we were able to put in three goals in a two-minute time frame to take a commanding lead. We never looked back as we beat Kiski 5-0, with Fletcher scoring the hat trick and Nate adding the other two goals. We had a few fun celebration goals as we did an on-field photo shoot that the boys did in front of our bench. It was very clever and quite funny. It was another great effort by the team, the defense, and a clean sheet by Braden in the net. Next up, we were set to face Mars Area HS in the WPIAL semifinals.

CHAPTER 10

Stress = WPIAL Semifinal Games!

We were now down to the top four teams in the 3A WPIAL playoffs. The 2018 WPIAL semifinal was next for our focused and confident West Allegheny team. Last year, our 2017 WPIAL semifinal game vs. South Fayette was easily *the* most memorable game of our West A soccer careers. No doubt about it! Overcoming a 2-0 deficit, scoring with twenty-six seconds left in regulation to send the game into OT, and then winning the game in double OT. Not much could ever top that game, right? Fast-forward a year later, and I was wrong. It did get more stressful, more exciting, and more memorable.

Our opponent for the 2018 WPIAL semifinal was the #3 seed, Mars Area HS. Like our quarterfinal opponent, Kiski, Mars was a team that our seniors had never played during their high school careers. There were familiar faces on the Mars team as they had many Cup players from Arsenal, SCS, Riverhounds, and other teams that the boys played against over the years. Mars was a team that went undefeated in their section and had an 18-1-1 record. Their only loss and tie were to solid 4A opponents early in the season.

Though we knew some players, we didn't know much about this team. But we knew Mars was a strong team. I had heard some scouting reports from parents I know in their section. The report was they were very physical, not a lot of team speed, but very skilled. We quickly learned that this team was very fast, very skilled, and very physical-a strong team across the field.

I have watched hundreds of West A soccer games and other high school games over the years. I can honestly say that the West Allegheny vs. Mars semi-final was *the best* high school game I had ever watched. Period. Exclamation point! It had everything. An up-and-down-the-field pace that was spectacular to watch. Tremendous saves by both goalies. Some on-field collisions that took your breath away. An ending that was so intense that it took a few days for even spectators to recover. It left spectators breathless and emotionally drained. It left players physically *and* emotionally drained. As ESPN might say, it was an instant classic!

I also spoke to several people that attended the game, and 100% agreed with that assessment. I have a friend, Brian Eagon, whose son is an eighth grader at Mars, so they came to watch the game. He said that it was the most exciting game he had ever watched at *any* level. Brian Eagon was a former Division 1 player at Radford University, so he has seen a lot of soccer in his years. I also received several messages from people that attended the game that couldn't stop talking about how they will never forget this game. It was that good.

The game started out as a fast-paced track meet with both sides getting some early opportunities. Mars capitalized only three and a half minutes into the game off a corner kick and a nice header to take a 1-0 lead. Mars was solid off of set pieces and had players making aggressive runs to the net off of these set pieces. They were very athletic. One of their senior players, Shane Lisman, was quite an impressive player, especially in the air. Shane will be playing at Allegheny College. We found ourselves down early, but honestly, during these first several minutes, the game seemed to be setting up as an offensive battle, with the potential for some goals.

The first twenty minutes of the game continued on a torrid pace. Braden Wurst made a few tremendous saves from point-blank range to keep us in the game. West A had a few near misses as well. One of Braden's saves had a Mars player take a crossing pass and was one on one with Braden from eight yards out and the entire goal in front of him. Braden made a quick reflex save and caught the hard shot, which prevented us from going down 2-0. It was an amazing save. On our offensive side, Antonio just went wide off a set piece, while Nate took a ball from ten yards out that the keeper made a nice save on, so we were getting some good chances of our own.

With twenty-two minutes left in the 1st half, Jaxon Ervin crossed a ball to Fletcher Amos. Fletcher made a great athletic move and put one past the keeper to make the game 1-1. Fletcher celebrated with his signature back flip. Almost halfway through the first half, we were back to all square, and the game was wide open and physical. The fast pace and physical play continued for another fifteen minutes towards then end of the first half. Then, we caught a break.

When you play games at the high school level, sometimes referees can hurt you and sometimes they can help you. Our second goal was a case where the referees were our friend. A ball was played through the middle of the field to Fletcher Amos with about three minutes left in the half. The Mars goalie scooped up the ball at the top of the goalie box as Fletcher ran full speed towards him as he was trying to catch up to the ball. As Fletcher ran by the goalie, the goalie extended his forearm and hit Fletcher high in the chest. Now, it's something that I have seen happen dozens of times over the years and generally no foul is called on the goalie. But this time, the referee deemed it a blatant and intentional act by the Mars goalie, and West Allegheny was awarded a PK, as the foul occurred inside the box.

Honestly, if the shoe was on the other foot, I would have been livid! I can understand the Mars coaches, players, and fans feeling like they were on the wrong end of a bad call. But, that is WPIAL soccer for you. It's a game where the referees can impact the game. And this call was an example of this. Nathan Dragisich stepped up to take the PK and buried it for a 2-1 lead heading to halftime. An action-packed first half that saw us go down 1-0, and now we were up 2-1 heading into halftime with a lead.

Things also intensified after the PK goal as Nate Dragisich did his signature "T pose" celebration. The Mars goalie and center back took exception to this. Antonio Fiordilino stepped in and got in a shoving and shouting match with the Mars players. The game was now taking a step to being more physical as emotions and intensity were running much higher.

The second half started with some pressure and a few good scoring chances by West Allegheny, but a counter attack by Mars five minutes into the second half and a nice cross tied the game at 2-2. Not much Braden could do about it, just a solid goal by Mars. It was a new game early in the second half.

The fast-paced game continued, and with twenty-eight minutes left, Antonio Fiordilino put us back on top 3-2. A corner kick went to Nate and he kicked the ball from the 18 to Antonio, who was standing about eight yards from the goal. It was hard to tell if Nate was making a pass or attempting a shot. The ball ended up at Antonio's foot, and he took a fantastic touch and made a quick turn. He drilled the ball with his right foot past the goalie into the right side of the net. It was a great goal by Antonio in a tight space within the box. A huge goal for Antonio and the team-could this be the goal that puts us up for good?

About seven minutes later, Mars answered to tie the game at 3-3. As Braden came out and slid to make a save and scoop the ball, the ball bounced away and was recovered by the Mars forward. The Mars forward made a shot at a very tough angle to put the game back at square. It was an unlucky play for us, as Braden had the ball in his grasp, but was sliding hard with the risk of going outside the goalie box with the ball. The Mars player, to his credit, never gave up, and the angle of his shot was very difficult. Just a solid goal by the Mars player.

The last twenty minutes of regulation saw both teams with great opportunities off of set pieces, crossing passes, and through balls. The game continued on a torrid pace and left the crowd gasping many times. One thing was apparent, and that was the boys, on both sides, were in great condition. As regulation ended and overtime began, you started to wonder who would be in better running shape. Who would muster up the energy to continue this pace for potentially another thirty minutes of OT, if needed? Much to the delight of the fans, the pace did not slow down in OT.

Both sides had great chances to win. During the first OT period, it looked like West A would come away with the win. Midway through the first OT, a ball was crossed into the box by Fletcher Amos. It was deflected by Benny Farelli to Evan Blunkosky as he ran towards the ball. He blasted a shot from fifteen yards out. The ball went past the goalie and it looked like we had the win. However, Mars player, Shane Lisman, was playing on the back line, reached with his foot, and just got enough of the ball to deflect it outside of the right post. The West A boys threw their hands onto their heads as they felt it was the game-winner. An amazing play by Lisman to rob West A of the goal.

During the second OT period, it looked as though Fletcher Amos had a breakaway as he ran towards a through ball and got behind the

Mars defense. At the same time, the Mars GK came off his line and was sprinting towards the ball. Fletcher was running at full speed and the Mars GK was as well. The two players came together twenty-five yards from the goal in what can only be described as a linebacker-meets-running-back collision. The impact sent a loud gasp and a loud *oooohhhh* sound from the crowd. Both players took the brunt of this hit and stayed down for a few minutes. There was great concern that the players could be hurt badly. It was a *really* bad collision. The crowd was silent as the boys laid on the ground in pain.

The trainers from both teams rushed onto the field. Luckily, both players got to their feet and seemed to be OK after a few minutes. Both sides breathed a sigh of relief that Fletcher was OK, and that the Mars goalie was also OK. Fletcher and the Mars goalie had played a heck of a game up to that point. They each had to come out of the game for the injury, but both came back after the next dead ball.

As for the play, a foul was called on the goalie as Fletcher got to the ball first, and the goalie initiated the contact with Fletcher. We now had a set piece from twenty-five yards away. Caleb Miller lined up to take the shot from the middle of the field. He rifled a shot that had the height to go over the Mars defensive wall, and it looked like it had a chance of going upper 90. But a Mars defender leaped into the air and just got the top of his head on the ball and glanced it over the goal. It was a great strike by Caleb. As the second OT period was coming to an end, West A had two corner-kick opportunities in the last minute of play that came very close, but Mars held strong and we were not able to convert. We were now headed to PKs. A game that nearly took your breath away several times was going to come down to kicker vs. goalkeeper. Who would be the one to come away with the win?

At the high school level, PK's don't happen very often. In WPIAL high school soccer, the regular season games can end in a tie and don't go to PKs. Most teams don't get the chance nor do they really work on PK's. During the four years that this group of seniors played, we *never* had a game that went to PKs. We were in unchartered territory. Both goalies, despite giving up three goals in this game, had played tremendously well. Both had stopped several great chances, made key saves, and kept their respective teams in the game. Braden easily kept us from giving up another 3 or 4 goals, and the Mars GK could say the same thing. You hear this a lot in soccer, but both goalies stood on their head in this game.

PKs also put coaches in a position to make tough decisions. Five players are selected to take the first set of kicks. Who will be selected? What order will they be? Will players volunteer or will you select them? What if PKs go beyond the first five players? Everyone needs to be ready.

From a kicker's perspective, you can *never* replicate the nerves, intensity, and emotion of playoff PKs when you practice them. In practice, you don't have your heart pounding out of your chest. You don't have the screaming crowd with *all* eyes on you. *It is literally impossible to copy a PK situation in practice!* As a player, you pick your spot, hit it with confidence, and hope you find the back of the net. Most of the pressure is on the kicker. As a goalie, you make a guess as to where the kick is going and try to get a hand on it. If the goalie guesses correctly, he could be the hero. Generally speaking, *all* the pressure is on the kicker.

After a short break following overtime, both teams sent out their first five players to take the PK's. Mars stood closest to the team benches, while West A stood closest to the spectators. Each of the five players stood at midfield waiting their turn. The nerves of the players were no doubt off the charts. West A coach, Kevin Amos, sent out Caleb Miller, Jaxon Ervin, Nathan Dragisich, Gabe Haines, and Gavin Chappel to take the first five PK's. Mars was kicking first and sent their first kicker to the PK line.

West A senior co-captain and GK, Braden Wurst, stepped between the pipes in the first round. The Mars kicker connected and *boom*, Braden stopped the first Mars attempt as he guessed bottom right and guessed correctly. What a start for West A. Braden was fired up as he pumped his fist and lets out a loud roar in celebration. The West A crowd and the West A bench were going nuts as well. First up for West A was Caleb Miller. Caleb calmly walked up to the ball from midfield and waited for the referee to blow the whistle. *Bang*, he confidently placed his left-footed shot in the upper left side and found the back of the net as the goalie guessed wrong and went right. After round one of PK's, it was West Allegheny 1, Mars 0.

In round 2, Mars got one just past the outstretched hand of Braden. Braden guessed correctly, but the ball was just out of his reach. Braden looks very confident and was getting off the line quickly. He was making it tough on Mars. Freshman Jaxon Ervin walked from midfield, stepped in, and waited for the whistle. Jaxon went bottom right, but the Mars goalie guessed correctly and made a great save. After two rounds, it was now tied at 1-1.

In round 3, Mars stepped up to the line with Braden waving his arms. *Boom*. Braden dived to the right, but the ball was kicked high and went over the goal and hits the football field-goal crossbar. We now had a chance to take the lead. Nate Dragisich walked up to the goalie box and waited for the whistle. *Boom*. He kicked the ball towards the middle of the goal as the goalie dived to the right side of the net. Nate found the back of the net. After the game, Nate would say he actually miss-hit the ball and felt very lucky that it went in the goal. You could see him react as though he missed the shot. He put his hands on his head as to say, "Holy cow, I'm lucky that went in." Sometimes, I guess it is better to be lucky than good! After three rounds it was West Allegheny 2, and Mars 1. We were in control.

In round 4, Mars found the back of the net as Braden guessed one way and the ball went to the opposite side. Senior Gabe Haines now takes the long walk from midfield and stepped up to the ball. *Boom*. He kicked a low and hard shot that went just wide of the left post. Gabe puts his hands over his face in disbelief. After four rounds, we were once again tied 2-2. The emotion was incredibly high and there was an unbelievable nervous energy in the crowd as there was no longer *any* room for error as we entered the fifth round. From here on out, it was do or die!

In round 5, Mars found the back of the net as Braden dove to his right and the ball went left. Now, Gavin Chappel walked from midfield and stepped up with a *huge* pressure shot. Gavin must make it to extend PK's to the sixth round. Miss it and we lost the game. Gavin is a player that has always had a quiet confidence about him. He calmly stepped up and waited for the whistle. *Boom.* He buried it in the back of the net and pumped his fist in celebration. What a clutch PK. I can't imagine what Gavin was feeling as he stepped over the ball. But, boy, did he look confident. After five rounds it was now tied 3-3, and now we are past our original five PK kickers.

There were now more decisions to be made by Kevin Amos and the West A coaches. Each team must send out additional players to take the PK's. For West A, freshman Johnny Dragisich confidently volunteered for Coach Amos and jogged out to the midfield line with the West A players that had already kicked. Mars sent out their player for Round 6. The Mars kicker lined it up and hit it. *Boom.* Braden leaped off his line and makes a great guess as he dove to his left and stuffed the shot. Braden was incredibly quick on the shot, and it didn't have a chance. The West A crowd was in a frenzy. The West A bench was jumping around and was fired up. We had the advantage and were now going to kick for the win. Who will it be that lined up for this kick? The two options are on the field and it was either Johnny Dragisich or Braden Wurst. As Johnny's dad, I was truly ready to vomit as they were deciding who would take the kick. The emotion was off the charts.

Kevin Amos looked over at Braden Wurst and called upon Braden to take the sixth-round kick. Johnny would be next, if needed. Our four-year starter at GK, would now become the kicker. Braden, the young man that kept us in this game with his hands, could now win the game with his feet. *You could cut the tension with a knife!* The entire crowd had all gathered towards the scoreboard end of the field to watch these two great teams end a long battle. As I looked around, some parents were even too nervous to watch, with their heads in their hands. The intensity of the moment was almost impossible to describe. On the game film, a few people were standing in the press box, and you could overhear them. As Braden was a few seconds from taking the kick, one of the ladies said, "Oh, sweet Jesus!" as she waited for Braden to kick it.

I remember looking over at the boys that had all just kicked their PKs: Nate, Caleb, Gabe, Jaxon, and Gavin. Johnny Dragisich was also there as he would be next if Braden missed. Their arms were around each other's shoulders; their faces were like stones. They were physically drained from 110 minutes of soccer. They now looked emotionally drained as their season and a trip to Highmark came down to one kick. The game was out of their hands, and they could only watch. Make it and we win; miss it and it goes to a round 7 with Johnny Dragisich up next and Braden heading back into the net.

Braden stepped up to the line, and the referee blew the whistle. Braden moved towards the ball. *Boom*. Braden went bottom right. The Mars goalie guessed correctly. *Bang*. The ball just sneaked by the goalie and hit the back of the net! *Wow*. The celebration was in full force! The West A bench sprinted onto the field, and the players who were lined up at midfield sprinted towards the goal and mobbed Braden, as he had just saved the game for West Allegheny, both with his GK hands and now with his feet. The West A crowd was out of our minds as we yelled, shouted, cried, screamed, and hugged anyone in our area! It was complete chaos. I ran over to Doug Wurst and gave him a big hug. I looked at Erin Wurst as tears streamed down her face and gave her a big hug as well. What a special moment for the Wurst family and our team.

Our Most Valuable Photographer, Sandi Miller, captured some great photos of this moment. In the background, there were shots of Coach Luke Navickas being almost tackled by Coach Johnny Aromando. The next photo then showed Johnny Aromando sprawled out on the ground as he fell down tackling Luke. Kevin Amos was looking on with a smile from ear to ear cracking up at what just happened. It was classic! Everyone at West Allegheny was overcome with joy. Our boys brought their celebration to the fence near the stands where students, parents, friends, and families joined to celebrate with the boys. It was a night we will never forget.

What an emotional game this was. Senior Nate Dragisich fell to the ground in relief at midfield after Braden made his game-winning kick. As Nate jogged back to join the team that gathered near the fence, he had tears of joy in his eyes and on his face. A young man that doesn't show a lot of emotion was overcome with emotion after this slugfest. Hats off to Mars HS, who gave us an amazing game. A game that we won by the slimmest of margins. A game that will go down as one of the best games that parents and supporters of West A soccer have ever seen.

Braden was our undisputed man of the match, and it will be a game that will be remembered forever. During his "man of the match" interview, Braden spoke about the final kick and how he didn't want to overthink the shot. Pick a spot and hope for the best. That is certainly what Braden did. Braden was amazing in this game. This was the game of Braden Wurst!

What is it about WPIAL semi-final games? South Fayette HS in 2017, Mars Area HS in 2018. Both games have given West Allegheny soccer families moments that we will *never* forget. I told many people that the boys will tell their kids and grandkids about these games. This group will be grown men in their twenties, thirties, forties, fifties, and beyond, and I'll guarantee that they will talk about these two WPIAL semifinal victories over South Fayette and Mars HS.

These are the forever moments. This is the reason you play. These are the memories that will be with you for the rest of your life. *It's just awesome*! Not many teams can say they have witnessed these moments. The fact that we have multiple times is very special. It was now onto Highmark Stadium for the 2018 WPIAL championship.

It was the match that everyone was expecting. #1 vs. #2 in the WPIAL, an undefeated team with one tie in Franklin Regional vs. a one-loss West A team. Franklin Regional had an easier time in their semifinal matchup with a 5-1 win over Thomas Jefferson HS. We had a quick turnaround for this WPIAL final game. The WPIAL championship was a Thursday evening, and we played Mars on Tuesday. After our marathon double overtime and PK game vs. Mars we had less than forty-eight hours to recover. How would we respond after such an emotional game just two days before? Highmark Stadium was the venue, and it was a great atmosphere for soccer. Many students attended the game, and the parents had a pre-game tailgate. The boys were ready to go, and we felt that this would be an evenly matched game.

Franklin Regional plays a very defensive-minded game. They like to possess out of the back. The first half of the WPIAL final was the direct opposite of our semifinal game with Mars. It was a fairly boring first half with a slow pace. We missed a few opportunities as Benny Farelli had the best chance and put a shot just wide left that would have given us an early lead.

During the first half, Franklin Regional was being patient and very deliberate. Franklin Regional struck first though, on a deflected shot by freshman, Anthony DeFalco. DeFalco is a solid freshman with a bright future. It was a well struck ball, it deflected off of a West A player and went in the top left of the goal. Though we felt we had many chances, from my view, something didn't seem right with us. Our legs looked heavy; we didn't seem to have the same energy we had in the Mars game. I think Franklin Regional's style had something to do with it, but part of me still feels our legs were recovering from the Mars game. It's certainly not an excuse, but we didn't seem to be our normal selves. And guess what, on this same night Mars actually lost in their consolation game to a team that they were supposed to beat. Heavy legs? Who knows? But Mars' season was now over.

West Allegheny continued to apply a lot of pressure in the second half, but low and behold, we did not have an answer to the lock down defense that Franklin Regional was playing. As the final seconds ticked off the scoreboard, we had once again come to Highmark Stadium in the WPIAL final, and once again left as the runner-up in a 1-0 loss. The boys were devastated. I remember Evan Blunkosky walking out of the locker room and I had a simple message for the boys: "Keep your heads up. We have four more games left." I hugged Evan and told him my simple message, and he broke down in tears. These boys wanted this win badly, and this one hurt.

I know Nate was basically a catatonic zombie for the entire weekend following our WPIAL championship loss. The question became, "How will the boys recover from this loss?" I remembered what Tyler Graziani said after our first WPIAL playoff game against Greensburg Salem. He said there would be bumps in the road. Would this bump in the road become a roadblock? How would the boys regroup from this? We now had a maximum of four games left in our season, and the M7 had a maximum of four games left in their high school career. From here on out, a loss would end our season. Would we walk off the field in tears of sadness or tears of joy? How would the boys respond?

CHAPTER 11

The Road to Hershey!

Here we were-the 2018 PIAA playoffs. Sixteen teams were left in the state of Pennsylvania, and each team was looking to be the last one standing with a championship trophy in Hershey, Pennsylvania. After a tough 1-0 loss to Franklin Regional in the WPIAL championship, it was time to regroup. Our PIAA playoff started on the road against Bradford HS. Generally speaking, teams from their district are not as strong as the top teams from the WPIAL. But after a tough loss in the WPIAL championship, we were interested to see how the boys would respond to this setback.

We made the two-hour drive to the DuBois area. It was a cold and windy evening on a field that was pretty narrow. We came out strong and really dominated the game. Despite being tied 1-1 midway through the first half, we came away with a fairly easy 4-1 first-round victory over Bradford HS.

The sting of our WPIAL championship loss was officially behind us. Freshman Will Douglas put in two goals, while Evan and Nate each added a goal in the 4-1 win. Gabe Haines sat out this game with a hamstring injury. We hoped the injury bug wouldn't start biting us as we had stayed healthy most of the season. But this was a good win for the boys to get us back on the winning track. Three more wins to reach our goal and only eight teams remained in the 2018 PIAA playoffs.

Once again, we found ourselves in the state quarterfinals in Altoona, Pennsylvania. This time last year, we came to Altoona with high hopes, but came away with a 4-1 loss that ended our season to eventual state champion, Lower Dauphin HS. Last year we had a 1-0 lead through fifty minutes, but eventually got worn down by a better team that had several college-caliber players, and two Division 1 players.

Our opponent this year was Hershey HS. Hershey had beaten Lower Dauphin in the district finals this year and seemed to be a very physical team as we watched video of them. It was a frigid Saturday in November in Altoona. The temperature was in the low thirties, but it was a sunny day. We came out strong in the first half of play as our boys had control of possession and had several scoring opportunities during the first half. However, we found ourselves in a 0-0 tie with six minutes left in the first half, despite controlling the pace and possession.

Coach Amos felt we were doing a solid job controlling the game in the midfield and limiting Hershey's chances with our strong defense. He decided to move Nate Dragisich up to the forward position with Fletcher Amos with about six minutes left in the half. The decision paid off quickly.

With four minutes left in the first half, Nate intercepted a pass at midfield and dribbled down the middle of the field. He laid a short pass off to Fletcher. Fletcher drew two defenders towards him and snuck a pass back to Nate as he moved to the left to separate from Fletcher and the defenders. Nate took the pass in stride as the goalie came out to challenge Nate. Nate placed a low, left-footed shot that went just past the goalie and into the lower right side of the net. Nate celebrated with his go-to T pose, which became a common celebration stance for Nate. It was a great pass and finish from Fletcher to Nate. It was 1-0 West A.

We felt very good that we could go into halftime with a lead and some momentum. But we weren't quite done yet. With under a minute left in the half, we struck again and went up 2-0. Off of a Hershey goal kick, Nathan took a headed ball from Evan Blunkosky. It was a great play by Evan, who sprinted from the midfield area to win the ball out of the air. Evan's header was a line drive that went twenty yards up the field. Nate sprinted up the field and shielded off a Hershey defender and settled Evan's headed ball about twenty yards from the goal. He made a quick move to the left and made contact with the defender. The goalie was coming out to challenge the ball, and Nathan quickly cut back to right and snuck a low shot in between the defender and the goalie to find the back of the net. It was a huge goal and put us up 2-0.

The Evan-and-Nate combination that we have seen so many times over the years had struck again. Nate ran to the corner and slid on the turf. He quickly popped up to his feet where he and Evan hugged in celebration. It was a big goal for West A as it gave us some breathing room and a lot of momentum. At halftime, we were feeling good with a 2-0 lead. Our defense was playing strong, while Jaxon, Benny, Gabe, Evan, and Antonio were doing a solid job in the midfield. Gabe was coming off his hamstring injury and looked healthy and was moving well, which was great to see.

The second half continued to be a physical contest with a lot of fouls, and some missed calls by the men in stripes. Hershey was playing hard and by no means had given up. Off of a West A giveaway and a nice strike from twenty-five yards out by a Hershey forward, we gave up our first goal of the game. With twenty-five minutes left, we were hanging on to a 2-1 lead. By all accounts, we were still controlling the game, as we were possessing the ball well and still creating opportunities of our own.

Then, trouble struck West Allegheny. The last thing we ever wanted to see on the field became our reality. How quickly a game and a season can possibly change. A scary moment occurred that had everyone on the West A sideline and stands holding their breath. With twenty-two minutes left in the game, our senior leader and GK, Braden Wurst, leaped for a ball that was played into the box. A Hershey player was coming in hard and took Braden's legs out from underneath him. Braden came down hard, hitting head first while also hitting his neck and shoulder area. Braden would be knocked momentarily unconscious during this fall. As he lay on the field getting attended to by our trainer, Pete, a wave of concern took over the West A stands. We were very concerned with Braden's well-being. Head injuries are just downright scary, and all we could do was pray as we watched him motionless on the field.

From a game standpoint, we were also concerned with replacing Braden for the remainder of the game, which was a narrow 2-1 lead for West Allegheny. There wasn't much room for error at this point. The boys had to rally around our new GK. *Never* had we been in a close game with any other goalie than Braden in the past four years. Hershey knew this as well, and might have gained some confidence just seeing our senior goalkeeper being helped off the field. Braden ended up walking off the field under his own power but with help from our trainer. We were relieved that he was able to walk off the field. But it was clear that he would not be returning to the game.

Coach Amos and the staff now had a big decision to make. Our back-up goalie was freshman Trevor Day. Coach Amos felt that Trevor had been sitting in the cold weather all game, wasn't warmed up, and it would be asking a lot of a young freshman player to be called upon in a state quarterfinal playoff game under these circumstances. Coach Amos made the decision to go with senior midfielder Antonio Fiordilino to put on the goalie shirt. Tony is a 6'4", slender-built midfielder for us. Though not a goalie, Tony was warmed up, he is a solid athlete, and he stepped up and welcomed the challenge to finish the game off. *Selfless*! He also wore Trevor

Day's goalie shirt which was a bite snug for the 6'4" Antonio. Trevor stands at 5'5" and 115 pounds. Spoiler alert; this goalie shirt would be worn again in the near future.

With Antonio now in the net, the game opened up and was going back and forth with a lot of physical play. Up only 2-1, there were some very stressful moments along with some pivotal saves that Tony made for us. A scrum at the 18 led to a rocket shot by Hershey that Tony was able to knock away. He knocked it to a Hershey player and the follow-up shot landed comfortably in Tony's hands. That could have tied the game, I thought. Way to go, Tony! Another big save happened when Tony punched a ball away off a crossing pass that had several Hershey players waiting for it to come down. Big-time saves in critical moments during the game.

As we continued to mount pressure on Hershey, we were awarded with a free kick on a foul that was inside the box. Freshman Johnny Dragisich came up big as he battled to win the ball off a Hershey defender. Though the foul occurred in the box, no PK was awarded as it was called an obstruction foul. It still gave us a free kick from close range. It was a questionable call not to award us a PK, but it gave us a chance nonetheless. Nathan Dragisich took the free kick and placed a low pass with some speed on it six yards from the goal. Evan Blunkosky made a quick run and lunged with his right foot extended at the 6. Evan's foot found the ball, and it deflected directly up and into the top of the net for our third goal of the game. Another Dragisich/Blunkosky goal-and-assist combination. West A now held a 3-1 lead with under fifteen minutes left in regulation. We now had some breathing room.

As the boys celebrated this goal, I remember Evan Blunkosky running back to midfield and pointing to our fallen GK, Braden Wurst, who was sitting on the bench. It was a moment that was special. Our boys wanted this game bad, and during the last twenty-two minutes of the game, they were playing hard for their fallen goalie, Braden Wurst, and for their current goalie, Antonio Fiordilino.

The rest of the game, we hunkered down on defense. Caleb Miller, Justin Shaytar, and Gavin Chappel were playing solid on defense, as Benny Farelli and Gabe Haines were playing a more defensive midfield position. We did a great job of preventing any more real threats from Hershey. A few times, I even noticed our midfielders, Evan, Jaxon, and Nate, close to the goal to help out their friend Antonio. Our boys made sure Tony was protected in the net.

The game ended with a great 3-1 victory over Hershey. As I interviewed our man of the match, Antonio Fiordilino, he talked about the need to do whatever it takes to help the team win. I'm sure the last thing he thought he would be playing on this day was goalie. A truly selfless act by a senior that stepped up big in a big-time game. Braden walked off the field, and there was a lot of concern on the players' faces, coaches' faces, and parents' faces. First, we were happy to see Braden walking around and talking. It looked like he was going to be OK. But he had his bell rung, and we were pretty sure that concussion protocol was in his future.

Around the same time that our game ended, we learned that Franklin Regional had just won their quarterfinal game. We were on a crash course to play them in the PIAA state semifinals. Would we be playing without Braden starting in the net for the first time in four years? Braden's health was first priority. Deciding who would be replacing Braden if he couldn't play was the next priority.

CHAPTER 12

Enter Gabe Haines!

After an emotional PIAA quarter-final win over Hershey HS, the team was playing extremely well and was once again bursting with confidence. Four teams remained in the state. What team would step up their play and go 2-0 to end their season? West A entered the semifinal game with a *huge* question mark. For the first time in four years we had to play someone at goalie other than Braden Wurst. Braden indeed suffered a concussion during the Hershey game, and would not be able to play in the state semifinals. There was even a possibility that he would not play in the state finals if we found a way to win the semifinal game. It was stressful times. Our Saturday win over Hershey gave us only two full days to prepare for our Tuesday match against Franklin Regional.

We had the rematch we were hoping for against the team that beat us in the WPIAL finals just over a week ago. Though the team was playing great, we now had a *big* question mark at GK. On Sunday and Monday, Coach Amos, Coach Navickas, Coach Johnny, and Coach Derek worked out different players and ultimately came to a decision. Though Antonio stepped in and played great in the win over Hershey when Braden was injured, the coaches decided to give the starting nod to another M7 senior, Gabe Haines.

Let's talk about Gabe for a moment. Gabe is a great kid, and a well-liked player on the team. He keeps the boys loose. He's someone that when you see the group talking, you see people laughing when Gabe speaks. Gabe has a great sense of humor and, like all our senior class, is a selfless kid. Gabe had been playing very well as holding midfield, and at times, he also moved to the forward position. He is a versatile player. Gabe had to sit out the first game of the state playoffs due to a hamstring injury, and he seemed fully recovered from it. But the decision to put Gabe in the net was based on his athleticism, calm on-field demeanor, strong leg on goal kicks, and leadership. Gabe is a very skilled player, so the boys were more than comfortable playing the ball back to Gabe and using him as an extra set of feet on the field.

Coach Amos tells a funny story of being interviewed prior to the State semi-final game. The interviewer asked Kevin about Braden's injury, and Kevin informed them of Braden not playing. He then asked Coach Amos about who was filling in for Braden. Kevin was telling them about the decision to play Gabe. He was asked about Gabe's experience at GK. "Um, this is his first game at goalie," Kevin said. They asked if he played goalie in Cup soccer. "Um, no, he doesn't play goalie for his Cup team." The sportswriter then asked Kevin "How many years have you been a coach?" Ha ha! Well, sometimes you have to do what you think is right for the team, and our coaches and players had the utmost confidence in Gabe. No one knows their players better than our great coaching staff. Kevin's message to Gabe was simple: "Gabe, tonight, you can only be the hero."

The PIAA state semifinal game against Franklin Regional was being played at Fox Chapel HS. It was another cold night in November. A lot of fans were in attendance to support both sides, and there was a lot of energy at the stadium and in the crowd. Even soccer fans not associated with either team came to watch this game, as it was a matchup of two very strong teams. These were arguably the two best times in the entire WPIAL in all divisions. One media person, Ed Thompson, even described this as the state championship game, as he felt the WPIAL was much stronger than the teams in East PA this year.

So, Gabe was in, Braden was in street clothes, and we wondered how the boys would respond. Also, Gabe decided to wear freshman goalie Trevor Day's goalie shirt. It was the same blue goalie shirt that Antonio had worn during the Hershey game. Once again, it was quite snug on the 6'2" Gabe Haines. That jersey should be framed!

It was game time. What fate would await our boys? From the opening whistle, we played with an energy level that I had not seen before. The energy was extraordinarily higher than we saw in the WPIAL championship game. Our legs looked fresh and we were buzzing around the field.

We were flying around, putting pressure on Franklin Regional, and we completely controlled the first half. But, despite that control, we were unable to find the back of the net and found ourselves in a scoreless tie midway through the first half. Right around the twenty-minute mark in the first half, a controversial call went against us. Off of a throw in, Will Douglas headed a ball to a streaking Fletcher Amos just outside the goalie box. Fletcher had a step on a defender in the box, and it looked like the defender clipped Fletcher's foot. Fletcher went down hard in the goalie box. The referee blew the whistle in what looked like would be a foul in the box and a PK for West A. However, this referee saw it differently and called Fletcher for an "intentional flop." It looked like a foul from the stands and on the video replay. But, again, this is WPIAL/PIAA soccer, and sometimes the calls don't go your way. Fletcher was given a yellow card on the play. In my opinion, it was a horrible call. Horrible is actually too kind of a word.

As we moved deeper into the first half, it stayed a scoreless defensive battle. Franklin Regional is a great defensive team, so it wasn't a surprise that the game was going this way. But we were definitely controlling the pace of the game, and had the better opportunities of the two teams. Our defense was also doing a great job, and though Gabe wasn't called upon yet to make any game changing saves, he made the saves he needed to make, and he looked extremely comfortable being used as an extra set of feet. We went into halftime in a scoreless tie.

The second half was a continuation of the first. We clearly were the better team on the field. Five minutes into the half, we had a great scoring opportunity. Jaxon Ervin crossed a pass to Evan Blunkosky streaking down the right side of the field. Evan made a fabulous touch on the crossing pass and put the ball to his feet running at full speed. He blasted the ball with his left foot as he fell to the ground. The shot was stopped by the diving Franklin Regional goalie. Evan got to his feet and got a toe poke off of the rebound that once again was stopped by the goalie. The goalie made a heck of a save on Evan. It was a great opportunity, and it felt like the momentum was firmly in our favor.

We were now getting some great scoring chances, but we were still scoreless through forty-seven minutes. Then, a momentum changer and Fletcher Amos struck. Fletcher capitalized on a bad pass from the Franklin Regional defense as they attempted to play a pass back to the goalie. The pass was miss-hit, and the speedy Fletcher outran the defender and took possession of the ball thirty yards from the goal. He shook off a defender and cut back to his right. He was at the end of the goalie box in the middle of the field. As the goalie was standing ten yards outside the net and another defender was bearing down on him, Fletcher placed a perfect shot that went just inside the right post and into the back of the net to give us a 1-0 lead. It was a huge goal by Fletcher. He celebrated in style with his vintage back flip. The West A fans were thrilled, our bench was jumping with excitement, and our boys were energized as they all came and hugged Fletcher. We had our first lead of the game with thirty-three minutes left in the game.

However, our 1-0 lead lasted only eight minutes as Franklin Regional scored on a set piece from thirty-five yards out to tie the game at 1-1. The set piece ball hit a head, skipped in the air and to the left area of the goal box. It found the head of a Franklin Regional player who headed the ball into the back of the net. Not much Gabe or our defense could do about it. The ball bounced to where they were and where we weren't. It was a new game with twenty-three minutes left in the game.

The one thing that many West A fans and players remember is how Franklin Regional celebrated this goal. The goal scorer ran by his own bench, stood at midfield, and looked at our crowd and at the West A bench and put his finger to his lips-ssshhhh. It irked many people and certainly pissed off our players. But hey, this was soccer and celebrations are allowed. We do T poses, flips, and baseball slides. But I don't ever remember us taunting the other team's fans. They had celebrated their only goal of the WPIAL championship in the same fashion. Boy, would a win be the ultimate payback.

The final twenty minutes saw us continue to pressure Franklin Regional. We continued to win 50/50 balls. We gave Franklin Regional very little room, and we seemed to be a step faster and just downright better than Franklin Regional. Anyone that watched the game could see that. A coach from the Pittsburgh Riverhounds Academy, Niko Katic, attended the game. Niko is a great guy, is a former professional player from Croatia, and coaches many of our players, including Nate, Fletcher, Caleb, Gabe, Johnny, and Mason. He commented after the game how West A totally dominated Franklin Regional. But would we be able to score another goal on their stingy defense?

On the West A defensive side, our back line of Justin, Caleb, and Gavin were playing a fantastic game. I also thought Benny Farelli had the game of his life. He was flying around the holding midfield position and helped to limit any chances that the Franklin Regional forwards attempted. Our whole defense was tremendous, but Benny was so good in this game. Benny missed the 2017 playoffs with his ACL injury, so it was wonderful to see Benny having this kind of game. Honestly, as I think back to the game, it was hard to even remember the Franklin Regional forwards being on the field. That is how quiet they were during this game. They had very little impact on this game. And these Franklin Regional forwards were very good players. They were the two leading scorers from Franklin Regional, but in this game, they were limited to not even having a shot on goal. They were virtually invisible in this game. Benny and our defense shut them down, plain and simple.

While our defense was playing rock solid, Franklin Regional had a very stingy defense as well. They had not given up more than one goal in a game all year. In order to win, we would have to do what no team had done all season. Could we score two goals on Franklin Regional? You started to wonder, would we be heading into OT? Could this be another game that went to PK's? It is now known that if the game went to PK's, senior Evan Blunkosky would be the man to stand in the net and play the GK position-another selfless act by a senior leader. Would it come to that?

With four minutes left in the game, we made sure it didn't come to that. Franklin Regional had a goal kick, and the goalie placed the ball down. He booted it fifty yards away from the goal, and Jaxon Ervin won the ball and headed it in the air. It went to a FR player standing forty-five yards from the goal, skipped off the Franklin Regional player's leg, and into the center of the field about forty yards from the FR goal. Nathan Dragisich raced side by side with a FR midfielder and won the ball while holding the defender off with his right shoulder. Nate then made a quick cut to his left, and then another quick cut to his right as he gained three yards of separation from the FR player.

Nate looked up and had Johnny Dragisich fifteen yards up the field to his left, and Fletcher Amos was about seven yards up the field to his right. He also had four Franklin Regional players in front of him, waiting for any through ball. Space was limited. As Nate looked up, Fletcher began to make a run down the right-middle of the field. Nate placed a hard grounder pass that cut through all four defenders as they gave chase. The FR goalie, the four defenders, and Fletcher all raced towards the ball, while Johnny Dragisich sprinted down the left side. Fletcher was in top running gear as he was twenty yards from the goal. He beat the Franklin Regional defender to the ball as the FR goalie sprinted out from the goal. In perfect stride, Fletcher got his right foot on the ball and placed a beautiful shot past the goalie, who was sliding towards Fletcher's feet. The ball snuck by the goalie and into the left-bottom corner of the net to give us a 2-1 lead.

It was a pass-and-goal combination from Nate to Fletcher that received praise from everyone that watched live, viewed the game online, or saw the replay afterward. One West Allegheny parent, Dave Cooper, whose son Brandon played a few years of soccer for West A, sent me a text and said that Brandon described the goal as something he had only seen in the English Premier League. It was that awesome!

A tremendous pass and finish by Nate and Fletcher. As Fletcher scored, he ran to the far corner, slid on the turf, popped up, and pumped his fist with a loud roar. Our bench was chaos as they jumped with loud screams and hugged each other in celebration. Our coaches pumped their fists and were hugging and high-fiving. The boys on the field celebrated this goal with class. You could even tell that Fletcher was overcome with emotion after his second goal of the game. This was no doubt the biggest goal of Fletchers career, and he was having the game of his life, scoring both West A goals in a 2-1 game. We now had a lead, and time was running down. We were feeling good and had about four minutes to shut Franklin Regional down.

With about three minutes left in regulation, Franklin Regional had a dangerous cross that had us scared in the stands, but the cross hit an FR player and went out of bounds for a West A goal kick. You could tell Gabe had some adrenaline running through his veins as this goal kick went way past midfield. His goal kick easily went sixty-five yards in the air. Our replacement goalie was fired up and looking to be undefeated as a West Allegheny goalie. For the remainder of the game, there were no real challenges mounted by Franklin Regional.

In those last three minutes, each time we cleared the ball the noise of the West A faithful grew louder and louder. As time ticked away, the bench, the coaches, the players, and the parents were all in a frenzy. The clock struck 0:00 and we had won 2-1. The boys hugged, screamed, ran around, and cheered as we were now headed to Hershey for the state championship and got revenge over a very good Franklin Regional team. I did post a "Ssshhh" message on

Twitter to no one in particular. Ha ha! I have to admit, it was very satisfying to send this Franklin Regional team into the offseason with their first loss of the season. During our annual Night at the Races fund raiser, there were a few horse names that were "SSSHHHH, Franklin Regional." It was fantastic. I have a feeling a new rivalry was started in 2018 with Franklin Regional.

The men of the match were easy: Fletcher Amos and Gabe Haines. Gabe came into this game never playing the goalie position in his high school career. Fletcher had just scored two goals on a previously undefeated team that had not given up more than one goal in a game during the entire season. Gabe spoke selflessly as he described, "doing whatever he could to help the team win." Fletcher was almost at a loss for words as he said he had never been more excited to play in a game than he would be for the state championship.

It was an emotional win for our boys, and you could see the relief and happiness all over their faces. This was the biggest win of their high school careers. Oh, by the way, the Haines family is now the proud owner of Trevor Day's lucky blue goalie shirt. A deal was worked out, and I believe Dave and Kristin Haines will be saving the shirt as a forever souvenir from Gabe's goalkeeper victory.

West A did it; we avenged our WPIAL championship loss and now got to play one more game. There were two teams remaining, and a trip to Hershey for the PIAA state championship awaited our West Allegheny soccer boys. Everything this team worked for would come down to this. Eighty more minutes of soccer wearing a West Allegheny uniform remained. Our M7 group would play *one more* game in their high school soccer careers. Would they walk off the field for the last time in a happy frenzy, or in tears of sadness?

CHAPTER 13

Hershey Bound!

An emotional and dominant 2-1 semi-final win over Franklin Regional sent us to Hershey Park Stadium for the Class 3A PIAA state finals. Our semifinal game was played on a Tuesday, and our state championship game was on Friday evening, November 16th, 2018. We had two days to prepare. We then had a travel day to Hershey on Friday. We were still over the top excited about our 2-1 revenge victory over Franklin Regional. Many writers on Twitter and other high school sports websites talked about the great game they witnessed and how well West A was playing in the PIAA playoffs. Some even said that they felt the semifinal match vs. Franklin

Regional would be the eventual state champion. But we had a lot of questions to answer as we prepared to play Strath Haven HS from the suburbs of Philadelphia.

We first had an important question to answer. What was the health of Braden Wurst? After sitting out a game against Franklin Regional for the first time in his four-year high school career, the big question was, would he be cleared and ready to play? Braden's dad, Doug Wurst, and I have had many long conversations over the years about the boys, our outlooks on games, and our analysis of games just played. I always look forward to speaking with Doug about this. However, this time was different. With Braden's injury at the top of everyone's mind, I didn't reach out to Doug, as I knew he was getting bombarded with calls and texts from parents, coaches, and others about Braden. I only asked Doug to keep me posted, and I simply prayed that Braden was all right. But if he wasn't, Gabe Haines showed he was more than confident and capable of winning a big game for us.

The plan for Braden was to visit the doctor, go through concussion protocol workouts, and pay a visit to the doctor on Friday morning prior to our departure. On Thursday, Coach Amos asked Nathan and Johnny Dragisich, Evan Blunkosky, Fetcher Amos, and a few others to come to the gym and put Braden through a workout that was being monitored by Pete Houdak, the West Allegheny athletic trainer. Gabe had also recovered from a mild groin injury, and Connor Blazer was slowed in the second half of the season by a nagging hamstring injury. Other than those, we were a healthy team. This was a big bonus as we played twenty-four games in a two-and-half-month period of time.

Thursday evening's practice time was scheduled at 6:00 p.m. In Pittsburgh, in mid-November, you never know what the weather will be. On our last practice of the year and the last practice of the M7's high school careers, our area received over three inches of snow that left the turf covered. Our boys were relegated to a film session on Strath Haven HS. They watched Strath Haven pull off an upset with a semifinal win over top-ranked Archbishop Wood HS. Who was this Strath Haven team? The boys didn't know anything about them.

Strath Haven HS has been long considered a soccer juggernaut in Pennsylvania high school soccer. They have six state championships under their belt. Their current coach won a state championship in 1995 playing under legendary soccer coach Mike Barr, who is in the Pennsylvania Coaches Hall of Fame. Strath Haven has a long tradition of soccer success, and we knew this matchup would not be an easy one.

As we watched film on Strath Haven, we saw them fall behind 2-0 at halftime, and then rally for three second-half goals to defeat Archbishop Wood HS in the state semifinals. Strath Haven is a physical team, a scrappy team, and a team that did well on set pieces. Our film session pointed out these strong aspects of this team to our players. But our boys were calm, confident, and you could tell they were excited for what awaited them in Hershey.

After a somewhat sleepless night of nerves, we had a Friday morning sendoff from West Allegheny High School. It was a very fun moment. Many parents and families were there to wish the boys good luck and bid them farewell. This would be the last time we saw the team until they were on the field in Hershey. The night before, several parents put together snack bags for the team's four-hour bus ride to Hershey. We took some pictures and loaded up the bus, but more importantly, we also awaited the results of Braden's doctor appointment and whether he would be cleared for our 6:30 p.m. state championship game.

I had asked Doug Wurst to shoot me a text with the outcome. Doug sent me a text in the morning that had a single word, "Cleared." A feeling of relief and joy came over me. Not just for our team, but I was excited that Braden could end his career just as it started, in the net as our starting goalkeeper. Braden was the last player to show up for Friday morning's departure as Doug and Erin drove him straight to the bus from the doctor's office. The boys were all fired up that their senior leader and goalkeeper was cleared to play. I remember hugging the boys and particularly the seniors, and I told them a simple message: "Have fun, enjoy this moment, and bring home a state title!"

Not surprisingly, this was our first ever game played on a Friday. Our games are generally on Tuesdays, Thursdays, and Saturdays. A lot was going on in the world of West Allegheny sports. Our friends at West Allegheny Football had a big WPIAL playoff game against Gateway HS on the same evening. It was legendary coach Bob Palko's last season as football coach of West Allegheny. Gateway HS was a huge favorite, but West A football is always well coached and has great players. Since there was a West A football game locally, we knew there wouldn't be a lot of students and fans making the four-hour drive to Hershey. As our game was at 6:30 p.m. in Hershey, a lot of non-parents and soccer supporters would have to leave work early to attend.

Our feeling was that Strath Haven would have a big numbers advantage in the stands, and it turned out we were correct. About five busloads of loud and noisy students were in attendance and outnumbered West Allegheny fans by probably 20 to 1. A group of West A students did make the trip to Hershey though. Our friends Evan Ferretti, Trent Johnson, Junior Bates, and Tanner Prevade, along with Kaitlyn Uram, Alyssa Goldstrohm, Grace Faulk, and Stacia Shaytar were all there to support our soccer boys. There were others that attended as well, and it was great to have some students there to cheer us on in the state finals!

It was a chilly night in Hershey. The day before, Hershey had been blanketed with about six inches of snow, a lot more than we received in Pittsburgh. As we showed up to the field, there were piles of snow six to seven feet high around the field. The stands were filled with snow as well, but the Hershey Stadium crew did a great job of clearing the stands out, and other than being cold for the spectators, the conditions were perfect for a state championship final.

Our boys warmed up and went through their pregame routine. We were ready to play and go after our first state championship in school history. The parents were a nervous wreck. The West A parents, families, and supporters gathered for a pregame beverage and meal at Troegs Brewery near Hershey Park Stadium. We could at least be a nervous wreck together! The game was being televised on the PCN (Pennsylvania Cable Network) channel. Families and supporters back home could see the game live. We were aware of several watch parties taking place back home in soccer families' homes and in some local restaurants. Celebrations Restaurant had a group of 15-20 people, led by my neighbor and childhood best friend Larry Zdinak. Chad Cantor, Harry Psaros, and Matt Dixon were with Larry cheering us on from Pittsburgh. They were shooting me text messages over the course of the game with some funny commentary from time to time as they watched the game on PCN. It was awesome to see such tremendous support from our community. It was now time to complete our journey. Eighty minutes remained in the season.

CHAPTER 14

The Final Game

West Allegheny and Strath Haven stood on the field facing the crowd as starting lineups were announced. You could see a nervous energy from both teams as they prepared to play in the state championship game. The national anthem was sung by a local high school student and we were now ready for game time. The West A boys huddled in a circle one last time with their arms wrapped around each other. Only eleven people know what was said in that huddle. I know the fans, parents, and friends might never know who spoke or what was said. Those moments stay between the team. This was it. This was what this group has wanted and worked for over many years. It was *game time*!

The game started with a fast pace. Strath Haven had the opening kick and put immediate pressure on us. Through the first 7-10 minutes, Strath Haven had us on our heels. They had a few solid opportunities with through balls that we were lucky to escape. One in particular had a Strath Haven forward with a break away as he got behind our defense. However, he took a long touch and the ball went safely to Braden Wurst for a fairly easy save. But with a better touch, he would have been one on one with Braden, and we could have found ourselves down early in the game. With a huge Strath Haven fan base in attendance, that would have been a huge momentum swing. We dodged a bullet early.

With 30:00 left in the first half, the game seemed to change. We moved Gabe Haines to the forward position with Fletcher Amos. We settled into the game and started possessing the ball effectively. We also figured out that Strath Haven was looking to rely on the "long ball" counter attack to beat us. We made some adjustments on the fly to respond to their style. With twenty-seven minutes left in the first half, we had our first great opportunity to score. Jaxon Ervin took a pass from Benny Farelli in the middle of the field and rifled a shot from thirty yards out that nailed the right post. It was a beautiful strike by Jaxon and was just inches from putting us up 1-0. But we were now controlling possession and had settled into the game and looked very confident.

The game continued to be *very* physical. A lot of fouls were being called, and the pace was fast. The early part of the game was reminding me of our game with Mars. Would this be another track meet? PCN TV broadcasters, Brian Keyser and Ari Bluestein, even commented, "Don't blink-you could miss a lot in this game!" Brian and Ari did such a great job with their commentary during the television broadcast. They had soccer knowledge, they did their research on both teams, and they knew the players' stats and knew some background stories of the game. Kudos to PCN for a job well done!

Both teams were flying around and being very aggressive. The crowd was also highly energetic. About 400 Strath Haven students now chanted, cheered, jumped, and made the stands shake at times over the first twenty minutes. It was a great atmosphere for state championship soccer.

At the 19:20 mark in the first half, a Strath Haven foul on Jaxon Ervin gave us a set piece opportunity from about twenty-five yards out, to the left of the goal, close to the sideline. Nate Dragisich lined up to take the free kick, while our midfielders and forwards, along with Gavin Chappel, were getting in position to find a way to get a head or foot on the ball. Nate placed a low floater to the six, where Antonio Fiordilino made a great run and got his head on the crossing pass from Nate. He powered the ball past the goalie for a 1-0 lead. Our boys were pumped! We celebrated our first lead in a state championship game. Fiordilino with the goal, Dragisich with the assist. The momentum was in our favor and we were fired up. The boys sprinted to the midfield area as they looked up to the West Allegheny stands to celebrate. High fives, hugs, and fist pumps were in mass quantity!

West A continued to dominate possession for the next fifteen minutes of the game. During this time though, Strath Haven had a great opportunity on a counter attack as a through ball split our defense and went to Strath Haven's leading scorer, Nate Perrins. He was just past midfield and was going to be one on one with Braden if he could catch up to the ball. Braden made a great read on the ball and sprinted out from the goalie box. With the ball thirty yards from the goal, Braden was able to beat Perrins to the ball. Braden's clearing kick hit off of

Antonio Fiordilino, and then deflected back off of Braden. The West A crowd gasped as Nate Perrins was still in the area and looked to find the ball. Luckily, Antonio was closer to the ball and safely cleared it out of our zone, and we maintained our 1-0 lead. A tremendous play by Braden to come out and hold Strath Haven scoreless.

We continued to apply pressure from the 15:00 mark through the 5:00 minute mark. A near spectacular highlight goal by Fletcher Amos *almost* made it 2-0 with nine minutes left in the first half. Freshman Jaxon Ervin, who played a tremendous game, played a crossing pass from the left corner into the box. Fletcher Amos, an acrobatic and athletic player, did a flying scissor kick and nailed the ball with his right foot in midair. Only a great reflex save by the Strath Haven goalie, Noah Atsaves, prevented the ball from going in the net. The PCN announcers were blown away by Fletcher's effort. Brian Keyser said, "You want to see dynamic, I give you Fletcher Amos...*wow*!" Both announcers were impressed and had a great reaction to Fletcher's near goal.

We were firmly controlling the game as we held a 1-0 lead late in the second half. Brian Keyser of PCN made the comment, "The Strath Haven boat is teetering, and they need to get to halftime just down 1-0, or they could be in a lot of trouble." Strath Haven was now relying completely on the long ball, as we were possessing the ball and controlling the pace of the game.

At the 4:30 mark, the game switched completely to West Allegheny's favor with a game-changing play. A foul by Strath Haven on Will Douglas gave us a set piece opportunity from thirty-five yards away. The ball was touched down by the referee. Nate Dragisich ran from midfield and noticed that the Strath Haven goalie and defense were walking slowly back to their positions on defense, suspecting we would wait to get organized for a traditional set piece. Some Strath Haven players were also arguing the foul call. Nate sprinted up to the ball, and a second after the referee touched the ball down, Nate struck the ball flush, surprising everyone. The ball was a hard-hit line drive and was heading for the upper-right corner of the net from thirty-five yards out.

The Strath Haven goalie reacted and attempted to jump and deflect the ball away, but he got there late. The ball hit the back of the net and we now had a 2-0 lead. Strath Haven was stunned, and West A was fired up. Nathan sprinted to the corner and did his signature T pose as every West A player sprinted up to do the T pose along with him. It was an awesome moment. Our players hugged, screamed, and were shot out of a cannon. The West A players ran back to the restart, pumping their fists and waving on the West A cheering section. We had now taken complete control of the game.

The PCN announcers highlighted that it was a game-changing play. Nate made a "high soccer IQ" play, according to announcer Brian Keyser, and Nate showed "great awareness," along with putting in a spectacular shot from thirty-five yards out. Nate noticed Strath Haven was not paying attention, and he took full advantage. It was a huge turning point in the game. Strath Haven's heads were hanging down, and we were beyond fired up. We continued to limit Strath Haven the remainder of the half, and headed into halftime up 2-0. We were forty minutes from our first state championship.

Strath Haven had been here before, though. Remember, we saw Strath Haven come back from a 2-0 deficit in the state semifinal game, so this was far from being over. We had to keep the pressure on them and we had to keep playing to win. Be aggressive-that was the message at halftime.

The second half started in a similar way, as we continued to control the pace and possession. Our defense of Justin Shaytar, Caleb Miller, and Gavin Chappel continued to limit chances and play tremendous defense. They had now adjusted to their counter attacking style and never allowed Strath Haven to get behind our defense again. Benny Farelli and Gabe Haines rotated in the holding midfield position and both played tremendous games. Gabe also played the forward position and was very effective up top as well.

With thirty-three minutes left in the second half, we gave ourselves some breathing room. Off of a Strath Haven corner kick, we had a counter attack opportunity. Gabe Haines made a great play to fend off a Strath Haven midfielder, win the ball, and play a forward pass to Nate Dragisich. Nate played a one-touch pass to a streaking Fletcher Amos just past midfield on the right side. Nate and Gabe both sprinted up the field, trailing the play to get involved in the attack.

Fletcher was one on one with a Strath Haven defender going down the right side of the field. The speedy Fletcher got a step on the defender as they approached the box, and he made a quick move towards the goal. The defender leaned in and clipped the foot of Fletcher and pushed him down to the ground. Fletcher fell hard to the ground and was in the goalie box. The referee quickly called a foul and awarded us a PK. A great play by Fletcher to draw this penalty. Strath Haven did not agree with the penalty. But the PCN announcers watched the replay and had no doubt that the right call was made and the PK was warranted.

Nathan Dragisich had been our PK guy all season, and he lined up to give us a potential 3-0 lead. This would definitely give us some breathing room. The PCN announcers said that this goal could put the game away. Nate was ready, and the referee's whistle blew as West A and Strath Haven players lined up around the goalie box, waiting for a potential rebound. *Boom*. The kick goes bottom right with a low line drive that never left the turf. The Strath Haven goalie guessed correctly, but Nate's placement was perfect, the kick was hit solidly, and it hit the back of the net for a 3-0 lead. Nate and the West A players all sprinted to our bench and jumped into the arms of our sideline players. It was a great celebration enjoyed by all our players, coaches, and supporters. Did we just seal the deal with that goal? Let's hope so.

As we held a 3-0 lead, the game opened up a bit, and Strath Haven was forced to push players forward. They had a few solid scoring opportunities as a result. With 17:30 remaining in the game, Braden Wurst made the best save of the game off of a great strike from Strath Haven. Other than his PK saves against Mars, it might be the save of his career. A Strath Haven shot from eighteen yards out was headed for the upper-right corner of the net. At the last second Braden reached up, fully extended, and just got a few fingers on the ball and changed the flight of the shot. The deflected ball moved a few feet higher, and hit the crossbar of the goal and came down to Gavin Chappel, who quickly cleared the ball out of trouble. It was a tremendous save by Braden and drew high praise from the PCN announcers. Brian Keyser said, "What a great save by Wurst!" He continued and said, "That save might get overlooked in a 3-0 game, but that was an incredible save by Wurst." Well, Brian, we agree! We will always remember that save by our senior leader, Braden Wurst. If Strath Haven had a pulse, it was quickly fading away after that save by Braden.

At the 12:00 minute mark of the second half, we put an exclamation point on the state championship game. We took advantage of a counterattack by Strath Haven as they were pushing forward, trying anything to get back in the game. Nate Dragisich intercepted a Strath Haven pass and settled the ball as it bounced off his chest. Nate dribbled forward in open space thirty yards down the field. It was 5 vs. 3, and we had the advantage. Gabe Haines was sprinting down the right, while Will Douglas was streaking down the left side, as Jaxon Ervin and Evan Blunkosky were trailing the play. A Strath Haven defender challenged Nate, and Nate laid off a pass to Gabe Haines. In stride, Gabe made a great one-touch crossing pass back to Nate. Nate took a touch on the ball and faked a shot that got the last Strath Haven defender to bite. Nate cut back to his left and placed a left-footed shot past the Strath Haven goalie for our fourth goal of the game. Off of a great pass and score from Gabe to Nate, we now led 4-0 late in the second half. Nate had just scored a hat trick in the state championship game. Our boys hugged and celebrated in a more low-key fashion, as we knew the state championship was firmly in our grasp.

The final excitement of the game happened with just forty-four seconds left in the game. A Strath Haven player that already had a yellow card and had about ten fouls in the course of the game was going for a ball near midfield. Evan Blunkosky was also going for the ball at full speed. The two met in a big collision, with Evan getting the best of this contact. The Strath Haven player flew to the ground as Evan stood tall. A foul was called on Evan, and an already frustrated Strath Haven team grew more frustrated and ran aggressively towards Evan. Strath Haven tempers were now flaring. The referees stepped in quickly and decided to give Evan a yellow card, mostly as a way to defuse the situation and not allow for any other bad blood with less than a minute left. Evan walked off the field to a huge ovation from the West A crowd. He yelled *"Let's go!"* as he received hugs and high fives from players, coaches, and school administrators. Evan Blunkosky put a final stamp on this game.

It was now celebration time! The clock hit 0:00, and we were PIAA state champions. The boys rushed onto the field and hugged, celebrated, laughed, cried, and were in a state of euphoria. Our seniors and coaches all hugged; as emotions were running at a high level, as our seniors played the final game of their storied high school careers. I remember Nathan falling to the ground in happiness and Evan came over and picked him up. They hugged for several seconds, almost in tears. It made me cry to see them this happy! We did it!

A fairly funny and somewhat painful moment happened during the celebration. Gavin Chappel took an inadvertent elbow to the nose from Coach Luke Navickas as Luke was hugging a player and caught Gavin firmly in the face. Gavin was fine, and we got a nice laugh out of it and are able to bust Coach Luke's chops about it.

As we lined up for the presentation of the state championship medals, the look on our boys' faces told the story. They had a look of complete satisfaction. A look of achievement. A look of a team that navigated a long twenty-five game season and would now end the season with a win and a state championship. I couldn't even imagine what our mood would be if it didn't end this way. Seeing the faces of these boys said it all. Seeing the faces of the younger players that didn't play but were able to go through this experience was special. They had a look of, "Boy, do I want to be here next year as well." This sets a standard that they will want to replicate in seasons to come. The freshman class learned a lot about being selfless, and the M7 set a great example for them.

The West A boys lined up facing the stands. One by one, they were given their state championship medals by Coach Amos. PCN

TV captured the happiness of this moment and our boys were smiling from ear to ear. Gabe made me laugh as he received his medal and looked directly into the camera with a loud *"Let's go!"* You can always count on Gabe for a laugh! After the individual medals were given, our four captains, Nathan, Braden, Evan, and Fletcher, were called to receive the PIAA team trophy. This was the moment they had all worked so many years to achieve. This meant everything to this group.

The boys raised the PIAA state championship trophy over their heads. The team gathered around for the celebration and photos. Many of the players kissed the trophy. A sense of pride was everywhere. Parents hugged each other and cried. Senior parents, the Wursts, Shaytars, Farellis, Blunkoskys, Fiordilinos, Haines, and Dragisichs knew that this would be the last time our senior boys would be on the field together. It was bittersweet and very emotional. You just never want these moments to end. Our boys had just left a legacy that will be unmatched in West Allegheny soccer history-our first state championship. It is only the third state championship in *any* sport in West Allegheny history. The blood, sweat, and tears that the boys put into this journey were now complete. We had climbed to the top of the mountain. We ended the season the way we wanted it to end-with a win, as state champions, and *unbeatable*!

CHAPTER 15

A Community Rallies

After the game, the boys took the bus to the hotel where the West A soccer parents were staying. We ordered pizzas, took photos, talked about the game, and basically took over the lobby of the Courtyard Marriott in Hershey. We celebrated for a few hours and sent the boys off to their team hotel so they could spend the rest of the evening together as a team. The long, exhilarating, and exhausting day was over.

The West Allegheny Boys Soccer Twitter account that I manage, @WestABoysSoccer, was blowing up with congratulatory messages. I sent a tweet after the game ended and simply said, "WE ARE... STATE CHAMPS." This tweet received 324 likes, and it was viewed by over 35,000 people! The excitement and news of our win was spreading everywhere. By this time, we also found out that our

West Allegheny football team had pulled off a monumental upset of Gateway HS, 42-28. It was a win that nobody expected. It was a great night for West Allegheny sports.

It was a touching moment when video surfaced of football coach Bob Palko talking to his players after their big victory. At the end of this speech to his players, he said, "And our soccer team won a state championship tonight." The football team cheered loudly. A few football players had played with us in the past, both in high school and over the years in the indoor leagues and WAYSA-boys like Connor Stout, John McCardle, Logan Malatak, John Rink, and Logan Scheider. Thank you, Coach Palko, for that shout out. We win as a school.

The next day, Saturday, the team bus headed home from Hershey. The bus pulled off at the Tonidale exit about five miles from West Allegheny High School. Awaiting the team bus were fire trucks, ambulances, and police cars from our area. They were prepared to give the boys a loud escort down Old Steubenville Pike to let our supportive community know that our state champs had returned home. Parents, families, students, football coaches, school administrators, friends, and others awaited our arrival at West Allegheny High School.

I got chills as the blaring sirens came closer to those awaiting our team at the school. The boys exited the bus to loud cheers and ovations from their friends, families, teachers, and students. We took pictures of the boys on the fire truck and had some great photo moments with our state championship trophy, medals, and our five-pound victory Hershey chocolate bar! There were wonderful articles written about our state championship game in the *Post-Gazette*, the *Tribune Review*, and the *Beaver County Times* highlighting our tremendous achievement.

The day before Thanksgiving break our school administration had a student assembly to honor our boys in front of the student body. Athletic Director Dave McBain said some kind and uplifting words about our team and our achievement. Little did we know, we would also be getting some national attention in the very near future.

CHAPTER 16

National Spotlight and Individual Honors

What else could top our state championship victory? We had reached the pinnacle of Pennsylvania soccer. You may be asking though, how are the boys viewed on a national level? Well, MaxPreps, a sports website that ranks high school teams across the country, reached out to Coach Kevin Amos and Athletic Director Dave McBain. They informed them that we were one of ten teams in the *nation* to be selected for the MaxPreps Tour of Champions. Not only were we PIAA State Champs, but we were also being recognized as one of the top high school soccer teams in the *nation*! It's too bad there wasn't a national championship tournament. It would have been interesting to see how our boys would do against the best high school teams in the country.

MaxPreps visited our school in January and presented us with the National Ranking "Tour of Champions" trophy and honored the boys with a video of our success. Each senior was interviewed and they posted the video on the MaxPreps website. The fairy-tale ending to our season was complete.

As the season ended, we also started getting some very prestigous individual achievements for our players. Nathan Dragisich led the way with some very special accolades. Nate had a big season with forty-four goals and twenty assists in his senior season. He was named the Soccer Player of the Year by the *Pittsburgh Post-Gazette*, *The Beaver County Times*, and the *Pittsburgh Tribune Review*. To top it off, he was named the **Pennsylvania State Soccer Player of the Year** and a **High School All-American** by the United Soccer Coaches Association. Nate was honored at the annual All-State banquet in Harrisburg. This was the first time in West Allegheny history that a player had been named Pennsylvania State Soccer Player of the Year. Finally, he was also named the Gatorade Pennsylvania Soccer Player of the Year. With the award, Gatorade donated $1,000 to a charity on Nate's behalf. Nate choose Open Field International, which provides access to soccer and life-training to youth in the country of Cameroon, Africa.

Fletcher Amos and Nathan Dragisich were named to the All-WPIAL team. Nathan was also named the WPIAL 3A Player of the Year. Evan Blunkosky and Caleb Miller, along with Nathan and Fletcher, were named to the All-Section team. In my opinion, we deserved more accolades from the section and the WPIAL. You never know how this stuff is voted on, but we certainly had players that deserved these accolades. I would assume that if you ask any of our players, they will take the *state championship* over the individual accolades any day!

CHAPTER 17

Where Did Unbeatable Come From?

As we sat in Hershey, Pennsylvania and were celebrating our win with the West Allegheny soccer families at the Courtyard Marriott, I interviewed our M7 Seniors in the men of the match postgame video. They had just won a state championship and were still glowing from the victory. At the end of the interview, I went around and asked each of them for one word to describe their state championship experience. Most of them said one word: *Unbeatable.*

You may be asking, where did this come from? How did this become the theme of the West A playoff run? It came from one person, Tom DeRosa. Now, you may be asking, who the heck is Tom DeRosa? Tom has been a supporter of West Allegheny boys' soccer for years. You see, Tom DeRosa was the soccer coach of Kevin Amos, Johnny Aromando and Elliot Constantine at Robert Morris University many years ago. He has maintained a tremendous relationship with Kevin, Johnny, and Elliot since college. Tom DeRosa is now seventy-three years old and still loves soccer. He is what I would consider an old-school coach. He tells it like it is, he doesn't sugar coat his thoughts, and doesn't believe in coddling kids. But, he truly cares for the kids he coaches. He is a breath of fresh air!

Since the M7 were freshman, they would get one or two visits to practice from Tom DeRosa each season. Tom would also attend a handful of games each season. Early on in their freshman season when Tom would attend a practice, it would start by the boys coming home and saying that they were annoyed by this guy who was correcting them, yelling at them, challenging them, and irritating them. I remember Nate Dragisich came home his sophomore year and said, "I can't stand that guy!" Nate was visibly annoyed by Tom DeRosa. Nate is a pretty even-tempered kid, so I wondered, who is Tom, and what was Tom doing to bring out this kind of emotion in Nathan? Kevin Amos filled me in on Tom and told me what got under Nate's skin.

Nate has always been a quiet kid. Kevin said that Tom noticed right away that Nate had some talent on the soccer field, but he also noticed Nate's shy demeanor. Tom was speaking to the group and he looked at Nate and asked, "Nate, whose team is this?" Tom wanted Nate to be more of a vocal leader. Nate certainly wasn't one to speak loudly or with a high volume. So, Nate said nothing. Tom asked again, "Nate, who is the leader of this team?" Nate looked around and shrugged his shoulders. Tom asked again "Nate, who is the leader of this team?" Nate said in a soft voice, "I am?", but not with a lot of confidence. Tom asked *again* in a louder voice, "Nate, *who is the leader of this team*!?" Nate, now a little embarrassed this time, said, "*I am!*" This was Tom DeRosa in a nutshell. He challenged our young players to be leaders. He took Nate and our boys out of their comfort zone, and Nate didn't necessarily appreciate that as a young player. I also remember hearing that Caleb Miller was not a big fan of Tom at first, saying, "I hate that guy!"

But it's interesting. Inevitably, the older they get, the boys all end up loving Tom DeRosa. Tom is passionate about soccer, knows the game, cares deeply for the boys, and he was a tremendous athlete in his younger days. Tom is like a drill sergeant that you grow to love! Coaches Kevin, Elliot, and Johnny have said many times that they have hours of legendary Tom DeRosa coaching stories. Kevin, Johnny, Elliot always say how they love when Tom comes to practice, as it reminds them of practices at Robert Morris University thirty years ago! They sit back and just watch Tom do his thing. As we entered the state playoffs, it was time for another visit from Tom DeRosa.

Tom DeRosa decided to stop by a practice as we were gearing up for the state playoffs. We were coming off a loss in the WPIAL finals and were still feeling the sting of that loss. State playoffs now awaited us. Kevin told me that Tom would be coming to practice. I remember stopping by this practice as I always enjoy watching Tom interact with the players. Prior to doing anything on the field, he gathered the boys on the opposite side of the field and was talking to them. Tom spoke to the boys for a solid twenty minutes. I asked Kevin, Johnny, and some of the boys what Tom was saying. It was a heartfelt motivational speech and he asked the boys some questions. "Give me one word to describe this team." Several players raised their hand. There were responses of "Passion," "Heart," "Dedication," "Skilled," and "Teamwork."

After many kids answered, Tom looked at the boys as they listened intently and said *"Unbeatable!"* You guys and this team are *unbeatable*! When you step on the field, be *unbeatable*! When you're playing in the state semifinals, be *unbeatable*! When you play in the state championship, be *unbeatable*!"

Well, it seemed to really have an impact on the boys. I asked the Magnificent Seven a question during the postgame man of the match interview. Give me one word to sum this day up and describe the state championship victory over Strath Haven in Hershey. *Unbeatable* was used almost across the board. It resonated with the boys. It sank in and made sense to them, and they certainly played that way in state playoffs.

Thank you, Tom DeRosa. The boys might not have been huge fans of yours at one time. But I know one thing. They *all* love you now. *You* are *unbeatable* to the boys of West Allegheny soccer.

CHAPTER 18

2013 vs. 2018

Over the years, I have become very good friends with our alumni from the 2013-2014 soccer team, watching them grow from middle school and high school boys into great men. Some have graduated from college and have landed first jobs. Some are still in school, getting ready to graduate. Zach Graziani got a job with PNC Bank and lives in Cleveland. Collin Wurst is getting his degree as a physician assistant. As I mentioned, this 2013 team had tremendous success in the past. There is inevitably a debate on what the outcome of a game would be if the 2013 team played the 2018 team.

What is even more compelling is that you have brother conversations that fuel the fire for this debate. Cooper Amos played on the 2013 team, Fletcher Amos on the 2018 team. Collin Wurst played on the 2013 team, Braden Wurst on the 2018 team. Even the Graziani brothers can have this debate. Zach Graziani played on the 2013 team, while Nate Graziani was on the 2017 team and played with every member of the 2018 team. And, of course, Kevin Amos coached both teams, and his sons, Cooper and Fletcher, played on both teams. This debate will be settled in this book!

This will be a fun debate, and we will have some fun and funny moments doing this mock game! First, I can't even begin to tell you how supportive our alumni have been over the years and specifically during the 2018 season. So many players came back to watch our games and support the boys. Collin Wurst, Cooper Amos, Michael Cummings, Nate Graziani, Zach Graziani, Tyler Graziani all made it to some games. I'm sure I am missing many others as well. Many of our alumni players wished our boys luck via Twitter during our playoff run. It was special to see this kind of support. Our coaches have fostered a great environment that gives our alumni a willingness to come back and support their alma mater.

So, let's take a look. The 2013 team made it to the state finals and lost a 1-0 game to Holy Ghost Prep. The 2018 team won a state championship with a 4-0 win over Strath Haven. Let's have some fun and do a quick comparison:

Record:	2013 – 21-1-3	2018 – 23-2
Shutouts:	2013 – 19	2018 – 14
Goals scored:	2013 – 80	2018 – 110
Goal against:	2013 – 6	2018 – 14
WPIAL championship:	2013 – 1-0 Win	2018 – 1-0 Loss
State championship:	2013 – 1-0 Loss	2018 – 4-0 Win

The Matchups:

Position	2013	2018
Goalie	Spencer Wolfe	Braden Wurst
Center Back	Zach Graziani	Caleb Miller
Left Back	Josh Kolarac	Gavin Chappel
Right Back	Levi Bergset	Justin Shaytar
Left Mid	Kyle McCracken	Antonio Fiordilino
Right Mid	Pat Harmen	Evan Blunkosky
Center Mid	Nick Jarzynski	Nate Dragisich

Center Mid	Mike Miara	Jaxon Ervin
Forward	Mike Cummings	Fletcher Amos
Forward	Collin Wurst	Gabe Haines
Forward/Midfield	Cooper Amos	Benny Farelli
Sub	Danny Aromando	Will Douglas
Sub	Daniel Heyer	Johnny Dragisich

This is a game of two teams with firepower on offense, along with the ability to shut you down on defense. It's a chilly forty-degree evening at West Allegheny High School, as the 2013 team takes on the 2018 team in front of a packed house. Tensions are high, stress is high, the Amos and Wurst families have been turned upside down leading up to this grudge match.

A small skirmish breaks out in pregame warm-ups between Fletcher and Cooper Amos. Fortunately, Kathy Amos came down from the stands and put a butt kicking on both of them. Thank you, Kathy! Prior to the game starting, Doug Wurst yells out his normal *"Let's go West A."* But who is Doug rooting for in this match? He says he just wants to see a good game. But we know what the love of a first-born child is like. Be strong Braden! Your mom, Erin, is rooting for you.

The game starts off as a physical matchup as the 2013s force the action up top with the three-headed offensive monster of Collin Wurst, Michael Cummings, and Cooper Amos. Early in the first half, after a through ball gets played to Collin Wurst, Braden makes an acrobatic save to rob Collin in the first chance of the game just six minutes into the first half. Braden has a few words for his older brother and wags his finger back and forth with the "no" sign. The trash talking has begun.

The game settles in as the midfielders of Benny Farelli, Jaxon Ervin, and Nate Dragisich control possession and the midfield. With twenty-five minutes left in the first half, off of a crossing pass from the foot of Antonio Fiordilino, Evan Blunkosky gets his head on a ball that looks like it is going into the bottom right of the goal. But a quick reflex by All-American defender Zach Graziani pokes the ball away with his right foot, and denies a great opportunity by the 2018 team.

In a 0-0 tie with ten minutes left in the first half, West Allegheny gets a break when Michael Cummings is given a yellow card for a cheap shot to Caleb Miller on a set piece. The foul occurs just outside of the box and the ball is placed twenty yards outside the goal. Caleb Miller, who has revenge on his mind for the cheap shot, places a perfect shot into the upper-right corner, just past the extended hand of Spencer Wolfe. The 2018 have a 1-0 lead. What a game and what a first half it has been. As we head into halftime, it is the 2018 team on top 1-0.

Kevin Amos spends equal time in the locker rooms with both teams. However, Coach Johnny Aromando and Coach Derek McCracken remain with their kids in the 2013 locker room as they leave no doubt whom they are rooting for in this contest!

As the second half starts, the 2013 team quickly shows that this game is far from over. Only two minutes into the second half, Collin Wurst takes a Cooper Amos pass and with some fancy footwork, goes bottom right to beat Braden Wurst to tie the game at 1-1. The game is getting very physical at this point. But the momentum has shifted to the 2013 team. Doug and Erin Wurst both clap for Collin, while telling Braden to "hang in there" at the same exact time. Collin is a pillar of class as he helps Braden up, but does serve up a wet willy to Braden's ear in retaliation for the finger wave earlier in the game.

With thirty minutes left in the game, the 2018 team looks as though we have another goal, but an offside call nullifies the goal. Kevin Amos is pissed, even though he still doesn't know whom to root for in the game. Derek McCracken and Johnny Aromando are thrilled with the call as they clearly would like to see their kids, Kyle, Danny, and Christian, on the winning side of this one, despite the fact that the 2018 team gave them their only state championship. Luke Navickas is keeping great statistics and yelling equally at both goalies, Braden Wurst and Spencer Wolfe.

Halfway through the second half the score remains 1-1, and it's about as evenly matched of a game as I have ever seen. Both teams have about eight shots on goal. Some great opportunities by both sides, as Braden and Spencer have both come up with big-time saves. With nine minutes left in the game, the 2013 team gets a chance as a crossing pass from Kyle McCracken finds the head of Michael Cummings and finds the back of the net. Cooper Amos does an amazing front flip in celebration of the goal, but Fletcher yells that Cooper's flips are mud, and Fletcher's are higher and more graceful than Cooper's. This goal by Mike Cummings is a possible dagger for the 2018 team. Remember, the 2013 team has only given up six goals all year. Can the 2018 team find magic once again? Doug Wurst leans over to me and says, "The 2018 team will get one more good chance."

Time is quickly running out on the 2018 team, and we have under a minute left in regulation. It looks as though the 2013 team is headed for victory in an emotionally draining grudge match of two West Allegheny titans. After a ball is cleared away by Zach Graziani back to the 2018 defense, Justin Shaytar wins the ball and passes to Fletcher Amos. Fletcher then passes back to Gabe Haines. Gabe puts a left-footed kick that finds Nate Dragisich, and he sends a pass to a streaking Gavin Chappel. Gavin moves the ball to the left corner and crosses a soft pass to a streaking Nate Dragisich. Nate Dragisich gets the ball ten yards out and is now one on one with the Spencer Wolfe. Spencer guesses and dives to his right, and Nate goes left to find the back of the net with twenty-six seconds left in the game!

Oh my Lord! It's like déjà vu all over again. Haven't we seen this before? The comeback we witnessed against South Fayette is replicated almost identically in this match. The crowd is stunned and chaos ensues. Though perfectly healthy, Kristin Haines decided to wear her walking boot, which she feels is a good-luck charm from the South Fayette game. It worked again! Kathy Amos doesn't know whether to cheer or yell, so she simply whistles very loudly. Kevin Amos does a soft golf clap to show his happiness for a great game that Fletcher and Cooper are both a part of. Assistant coaches, Johnny Aromando and Derek McCracken, are both incensed that their 2013 boys are now tied, despite the fact that the 2018 team gave them their only state championship. Luke continues to keep stats, and yells at Spencer for not coming out of the net fast enough and giving up a soft goal.

We are headed to OT. The rain is now coming down on this cold, wet, and chilly November evening in Imperial, Pennsylvania. The first overtime period sees a back-and-forth track meet. Nate Dragisich, Jaxon Ervin, and Fletcher Amos are putting a lot of pressure on defenders Josh Kolarac, Zach Graziani, and Levi Bergset. Levi, an exchange student, yells profanities in his native language, but no one really understands what he is saying. Cooper, Michael, and Collin continue to put pressure on the 2018 defense. Justin Shaytar, Caleb Miller, Gavin Chappel, Benny Farelli, and Gabe Haines are equal to the task though. No golden goal in the first OT period.

We now move into double OT with the game still knotted at 2-2. With nine minutes left in the OT period, Gabe Haines launches a laser from thirty yards out. Spencer Wolfe just gets a finger on it and sends it inches over the crossbar. What a chance for the 2018 team. Corner kick for the 2018 team.

Nate Dragisich lines up to take the corner kick. As the ball approaches, Spencer leaps up in the air. He seemingly has control of the ball. However, Fletcher Amos runs solidly into Spencer, sending Spencer in the air as he lands flat on his back. The ball pops out of Spencer's hands. There is a mad scramble for the ball. The 2013 team attempts to clear the ball. Justin Shaytar gets his head on the attempted clear ball and it lands at the foot of Evan Blunkosky. Evan turns quickly as Spencer gets up and comes to his feet. Evan launches a low screamer towards Spencer. The ball is soaked, the field is soaked, and uniforms are soaked. The ball goes through the waiting arms of Spencer Wolfe for a 2018 game winning goal!

Oh my Lord! What just happened here? It's almost a repeat of the best victory in the history of the 2018 team, combined with a repeat of the toughest loss for the 2013 team. Oh the humanity! Team 2018 wins 3-2 in double OT.

Doug Wurst is seen hugging both Braden and Collin after the game. He then whispers to Collin that the 2013 team is still the better team. Kevin Amos tells both teams separately that they are the better team, but just reminds them, "Don't tell the other team I said that." Derek and Johnny are seen binge eating the state championship five-pound Hershey chocolate bar after the game. Luke is tallying up the stats and wondering who is going to step into the goalie position in 2019. Kathy Amos, Kristin Haines, and Malinda Dragisich are opening their second bottle of cabernet. The Amos brothers and the Wurst brothers are both hugging it out. This debate will likely continue.

That was a lot of fun! In all honesty, I would love to see how this matchup would have ended. So many great players and, more importantly, great young men on these two teams. Two teams with a combined four-year record of 82-11-5 in the 2013, 2014, 2017, and 2018 seasons. Many players from these teams moved on to play college soccer. A lot of All-Section, All-WPIAL, All-State, and All-American players. It really does make for a great debate. One thing is not debatable. These two teams have set the bar extremely high in West Allegheny soccer history, and we will forever be grateful for these young men.

CHAPTER 19

Honoring West A and M7

With a magical state championship in hand, and a Max Preps honor of being one of the top teams in the entire country, West

Allegheny's soccer team success was complete. We also had some individual honors that were quite impressive as well.

As I mentioned, four West Allegheny players were named to the All-Section team. Nathan Dragisich, Fletcher Amos, Evan Blunkosky, and Caleb Miller all were given these honors. Only fifteen players are selected, and I felt several other West A players were worthy of this honor. Nathan Dragisich and Fletcher Amos were also selected as All-WPIAL players.

Nathan Dragisich and Evan Blunkosky were selected to participate in the All-WPIAL senior game at the conclusion of the season. It was fitting that Evan and Nate played their first *ever* soccer game as teammates at the YMCA at the age of four. And now the last game they would play as high schoolers, they would be teammates on the field. And wouldn't you know, Nate and Evan both scored a goal in the WPIAL All-Star game! A fitting end.

As we look at the M7 group, it is fitting that four of these boys will be moving on to play at the next level in college. Nathan Dragisich signed with Duquesne University in the D1 Atlantic-10 Conference. Evan Blunkosky signed to play at D2 California University of Pennsylvania. Gabe Haines will be playing at Marietta College in Ohio. Antonio Fiordilino will play at Geneva College, about forty minutes north of Pittsburgh. Truth be told, all seven of the M7 boys had the ability to play at the next level. Braden, Benny, and Justin chose not to continue their soccer careers in college. They will simply leave as state champions.

As I think back to this group of players, and of the entire West Allegheny 2018 team, I think of one word: *Selfless*. A team that was never worried about individual attention. A group that wanted to win a championship more than anything. A group that figured out early that each of them had a role to play on the team: some as scorers, some as defenders, and some as goalies, when needed! A group that knew that no one player was bigger than the team. A group that did whatever it took to win. A team that was made up of more than just teammates, they were friends and brothers.

We saw our boys step into situations that had to make them nervous. We saw these boys play at a high level all season. We saw them persevere through these moments. We saw them overcome obstacles. **These are your 2018 West Allegheny Soccer boys:**

Gabe Haines: He stepped up and played goalie for the first time in his high school career in the state semifinal game against Franklin Regional, and he won! He assisted on the final goal of the state championship game. He is headed to Marietta College to play soccer.

Antonio Fiordilino: Who will ever forget when he played goalie for the first time in his career in the second half of the state quarterfinal game, and won! He scored the first goal in the state championship game off of a beautiful header. He is heading to Geneva College to play soccer.

Justin Shaytar: A senior that cemented himself in the right back position and could always be counted upon to deliver in the big games. Always a positive attitude, and no one will outwork Justin-no one. He is headed to Rochester Institute of Technology to study engineering.

Benny Farelli: Mr. Versatility who played multiple positions during the season and ended up playing his best soccer in the PIAA playoffs-an unsung hero in our PIAA run. He worked hard to return from an ACL injury during his junior season and leaves as a state champion. He is undecided where he will attend college.

Braden Wurst: He put fear aside after a scary concussion in state quarterfinals and came back in the state championship game to put up a clean sheet. He had thirty-five shutouts in his GK career, a West Allegheny record. No one will ever forget what he did to lead us to victory over Mars Area High School in the 2018 WPIAL semifinals. He is headed to the University of Kentucky to study premed.

Evan Blunkosky: He will be remembered as a great leader, a great person, and the player that always sacrificed his body as he flew through the air to bang in a header goal. No one dominated the right-wing position like Evan did. Evan leaves West Allegheny with thirty goals in his career. He started every game in his four-year high school career. He is headed to California University of PA to play soccer.

Nate Dragisich: He saved his best for last in a storied West Allegheny soccer career, recording a hat trick in the state championship game. He led his team with a selfless attitude and humble nature. He was named Pennsylvania State Player of the Year, All-American, and leaves as the all-time leader in goals and assists at West Allegheny. He is headed to Duquesne University to play D1 soccer in the Atlantic-10 Conference.

Caleb Miller: Our junior rock at center back. A dangerous left foot off of set pieces, and a young man that has aspirations of heading to West Point or the Naval Academy. He led our defense to numerous shutouts over his first three varsity seasons. A smart and kind young man. The entire package!

Fletcher Amos: His athletic ability and speed make him so dangerous. He is a threat any time he touches the ball. He finishes his junior season as top five all-time in both goals and assists. He had the biggest game of his career in the state semifinal victory over Franklin Regional, scoring both goals in a 2-1 victory.

Gavin Chappel: He selflessly moved to play defense from his natural wing position in order to solidify our defense in his junior season. Never complained, and always focused on winning. A true "team first" attitude. Gavin will have a huge senior year and be a leader of the team in 2019.

Connor Blazer: He fought through a hamstring injury in his sophomore season, and he will be counted on to be a leader of the team as he enters his junior season. He had two big goals in an important early season victory over Quaker Valley.

Jaxon Ervin: He played like a varsity soccer veteran in 2018. He stepped onto a team that started ten seniors and juniors and started every game as a freshman. He made us a better team. Jaxon ended his freshman season with ten goals and eighteen assists. His eighteen assists are a West Allegheny freshman record. His future is bright!

Will Douglas: He started several games as a freshman and played valuable minutes in all our big games. He led us with two big goals in our first PIAA playoff game against Bradford HS. He will be a force over the next three years.

Johnny Dragisich: He played big minutes all season and also played big minutes in the state semifinal and state championship games. He will play wherever you ask him. He started one game in his freshman season. A versatile player and fierce competitor. He will be a big part of our team's future success.

To our JV players and other varsity rostered players that might have not seen a lot of playing time towards the end of the season, but were seen jumping around, celebrating, and completely into the intensity of each game: Your enthusiasm was contagious. Success comes to the whole team, and everyone plays a role. Your time on the field is coming soon.

This is *your* 2018 West Allegheny soccer team. A team that is selfless. A team that will always call themselves state champions. A team that leaves a legacy that will always be remembered in West Allegheny history. A team that lived by one motto: To finish the season as *Unbeatable*!

CHAPTER 20

Memories and Parent Messages

When I think back to these awesome and unforgettable moments that we experienced, I am thankful to have been a part of this journey. During the time I put these memories on paper, I also think of the many quick memories over the years that I remember from time to time-maybe not enough of a moment to define a season, but great memories, nonetheless. Here are a few extra moments that I will always remember fondly.

- Evan Blunkosky and Braden Wurst postgame victory poses. Evan and Braden always made it a point to find our photographer, Sandi Miller, and get a victory pose: Evan shining Braden's shoe, a picture of a jump in the air with a heel click. A great montage of pictures of these two camera-loving seniors can be found at Sandi's website, Blink of an Eye: Sports and Family Photography!

- I remember Mason Day assisting Nathan Dragisich on a goal. Mason Day is a freshman and is loved by his teammates. He is a late bloomer and is one of our smallest members on the team. During our home game against Montour, he assisted Nate on a goal. Nate pointed to Mason, ran up to him, picked him up, and put him over his shoulder as he started to run. Mason put his arms out in an airplane style. It was great! Sandi Miller captured this moment in a photo.

- I had the pleasure of spending a Shadow Day with Gabe Haines and Evan Blunkosky during their junior season as part of their school requirement. When I was with Evan, we met someone for breakfast, met with two other people for coffee and one person for lunch. At the end of the day, Evan said, "Coach Brent, you drink a lot of coffee during the day." I agree, Evan! During my day with Gabe, I took him to lunch with my clients at the Capital Grille. I saw a look of happiness as I told Gabe to order whatever he wanted. Filet mignon was the choice, and Gabe was loving it! Getting to spend the day and speak with these young men for a whole day was very special to me.

- I remember driving the boys to practice on a Saturday morning during their sophomore season. Justin Shaytar had just received his learner's permit. He jumped in my car, and I asked him about getting his permit. I then said, "You drive to the high school." Justin had a look of terror on his face as he responded, "Well, I've never actually driven a car on the road before." I told him that today would be his first time. He did great and had some white knuckles during the five-mile drive while Antonio, Evan, and Nathan sat calmly in the car.

- I remember the game where Johnny Dragisich assisted Nathan Dragisich on a goal-the brother combination! This was the first year that they played a competitive and organized game as teammates. After the goal, Nathan ran over to Johnny and Johnny jumped into Nathan's arms to celebrate. Once again, Sandi Miller captured this wonderful moment. This moment was witnessed by all four grandparents, and it was a moment that brought tears to their eyes. Very special!

- I remember our 2018 soccer banquet. After fifteen years of coaching, our long-time assistant coach, Derek McCracken, was retiring. There were many video tributes from former players talking about how much Derek and the West A program has meant to them. Kevin Amos paid a tribute and was emotional as he talked about the years of memories. Thank you, Derek McCracken, for all you have done for West A soccer!

- We love the Farelli family. There is nothing funnier than hearing Benny Farelli and the boys do a Jeff Farelli impersonation. You can't describe it in words, but I laugh out loud when I think about it.

- I remember when Caleb Miller sat out a game with a virus that was known to be contagious. Upon his return, the starting lineups were being announced. When Caleb's name was called, the player line chose to salute Caleb instead of offer a high-five or hand shake. It brought a big smile to Caleb's face and made everyone laugh-a great sense of humor on this team!

- I remember Tiffany Dragisich, the younger sister of Nathan and Johnny, joining the boys at a summer conditioning while they were doing a plank-off. She's a gymnast and is pretty strong. Who could hold the plank the longest? I remember

Gavin Chappel throwing grass clippings at Tiffany to try and stop her from winning. He had everyone cracking up!

- I remember another moment from our banquet this year as Evan Blunkosky spoke in front of the group. I remember his emotion when talking about his family and their support of him during his soccer career. He spoke about his friendships, and his love of his team. It was presented from the heart of a great young man. It brought tears to my eyes, and to many parents who were in attendance. You realize how important this team is to these young men.

- I remember looking at pictures of the M7 from their freshman year of camp, and then from their senior year of preseason camp. In the freshman year photo, they were young boys, their arms were behind their backs, probably very nervous about heading to their first camp. In the senior camp photo, you see mature young men, arms around each other's shoulders, standing side by side, close to each other, and standing with confidence as leaders of the team. Boys became men.

- I remember a tweet from West A class president, Tanner Prevade. Tanner is a good friend of the soccer players. When we left for preseason camp, I tweeted a picture of the West Allegheny team getting ready to depart. Tanner responded, "2018 State Champs." I think Tanner has magical powers! What a great prediction by Tanner. He was a big supporter of our team and attended many games. He will always be a part of the West Allegheny soccer family.

- I remember driving up the road in my neighborhood and seeing Evan, Antonio, and Jimmy Ervin coming down to my house. They were on their Segways. They were holding a large ladder and an eight-foot tall green alien blow-up doll. When I pulled up to them and rolled down my car window, they had a solid look of guilt on their faces. I asked, "Are you headed to my house with that?" They were busted, and quietly said yes. I looked at them and started laughing and simply said, "Please don't fall off the ladder." They laughed with a sigh of relief. Playing a prank on Nate sounded fun. Love those guys!

- I remember the boys having many bonfires in the neighborhood back yards during the summer. Evan, Nathan, Antonio, and Jimmy Ervin were all having great evenings doing this. Other neighborhood friends, and many members of the soccer team from other neighborhoods would join these evenings and hang out by the fire. They were team building and they didn't even realize it at the time. They were just kids having a fun summer.

- Here is my Top 10 list of West Allegheny soccer games that I witnessed over the last two seasons, from 1 through 10.

1. West Allegheny vs. Mars, 2018: 3-3 (4-3 in PK's)-Game of the year sent us to 2018 WPIAL final for second year in a row. Best game I've ever seen!

2. West Allegheny vs. South Fayette, 2017: 3-2 OT-Comeback of the ages sent us to 2017 WPIAL final.

3. West Allegheny vs. Franklin Regional, 2018: 2-1–State semifinal win got us revenge for our WPIAL finals loss and sent us to state title game.

4. West Allegheny vs. Strath Haven, 2018: 4-0–State champs! Dominated!

5. West Allegheny vs. Hershey, 2018: 3-1–Braden hurt, Antonio went in at GK.

6. West Allegheny vs. Montour, 2017: 2-1–Two Evan Blunkosky goals gave us a come-from-behind victory.

7. West Allegheny vs. Montour, 2017: 3-2–Another come-from-behind win to clinch the section title.

8. West Allegheny vs. Blackhawk, 2018: 2-0–After a red card, we played a man down for the final fifty-five minutes.

9. West Allegheny vs. Quaker Valley, 2018: 4-2–Beat the defending 2A state champs to set the tone for the season.

10. West Allegheny vs. South Fayette, 2018: 1-0–A scrappy win early in the 2018 season over our bitter rival.

Messages from Our Senior Parents:

Two questions were asked of our wonderful senior parents.

1. What is your favorite West Allegheny soccer memory with our senior class?
2. How would you describe the West Allegheny soccer senior class and what message to you have for them as they graduate from West Allegheny High School?

Kris and Kim Blunkosky:

1. While there are so many amazing moments you gave us through the years, your overall progression to state champion seniors is the most memorable. Each year, you improved over the next. As your wins and confidence increased, you grew as players and leaders. You remained coachable and continuously worked hard to elevate yourselves and your team. From the double OT win at South Fayette to the PK-shootout win over Mars to avenging your loss against Franklin Regional to the state championship win in Hershey, the evolution of each of you and of your team was remarkable!

2. You are truly a special group of young men. When your journey first began back in the WAYSA days, you learned not just how to play, but to love the game of soccer. From early on, you displayed great potential and a passion to win. Together, you became better and better through WAYSA, Sewickley Sportrak, Southpointe, STM, middle school, and eventually on to different cup teams. Despite what your paths and relationships were, the chemistry remained and you instantly bonded each time you took the soccer field together. No matter the team or the circumstance, you faced each challenge with resolve. You described yourselves as unbeatable, but you were also unbreakable. As a team and as individuals, you were resilient throughout your high

school careers. From injuries to tough losses, you remained unbreakable and came back stronger each time you fell. That resilience resulted in the ultimate reward-*state champions*! As you leave high school behind and begin your life journey, channel that resilience you had during your historic journey to the first soccer state championship victory in West Allegheny High School and apply it throughout your lives. With your character and resilience, there will be countless victories in your futures! Good luck!

Doug and Erin Wurst:

1. We have built many years of memories of this WA soccer senior class. We feel the decision that was made by the parents when the boys were only eight years old, to want to develop a winning West A team, was crucial to their success. These boys are friends both on and off the field, which made them such a cohesive team. We enjoyed coaching the boys when they were younger as well as watching the indoor soccer games at Southpointe, to even the late competitive nights playing the Numbers Game. We have witnessed these boys develop within their own club and come back each fall to their West A soccer family.

    As freshmen, they stepped on to the field young and naïve. They paid their dues, never got discouraged and continued to work hard each season. As Braden's parents, one of our favorite memories is winning the WPIAL semifinal game against Mars in penalty kicks. Outside of the state championship win, this was one of the most excited we have ever seen the boys, the fans, and the parents!

2. Determined, hardworking, steady, unselfish, motivated, and leaders are words that describe this team. These boys have known each other since elementary school and developed

a strong bond that has formed over the last twelve years that can't be broken, each one bringing their own style and personality to the group. This team always supported each other both on and off the field. The last four years, they focused their efforts on a common goal, a state championship win. We are so happy we were there to celebrate this huge accomplishment with them!

Best of luck in college or where ever your future takes you! Study hard and don't forget to call your Mom & Dad!

John and Marice Shaytar:

1. Our favorite memory doesn't just come at one exact moment. It is the entire senior season. Game by game, each of them full of excitement and emotions from each and every one of them. What a ride and quite the show!

2. Unique and blessed. An outstanding group of young men that truly support each other with a lifetime of memories. Friends for life. We are proud of the awesome young men they have all become. We wish them all the best of success and happiness in the next chapter of their lives. Stay focused and continue to have high expectations. There are no limits to success. Love you all!

Brent and Malinda Dragisich

1. The memories these boys have provided are countless. We remember the challenges, we remember the tears. But we will forever have the vision of these boys holding the state championship trophy over their heads in Hershey, Pennsylvania. Gathered as a group of boys that reached the goal they set out to achieve. The excitement on their faces and the overwhelming joy they had still gives us chills. We will remember the celebrations of goals and celebrations

after a big win. We will remember the boys hugging and showing such raw emotion after these victories, while also lifting each other up during the defeats. With Nathan, we will always remember how these games brought out a wide range of emotions in a mild-mannered young man: tears of joy after the Mars and Strath Haven games, complete and utter sadness after our WPIAL final loss. But seeing Nate in Hershey, bursting with happiness and surrounded by his closest friends, still brings joy to our hearts. Seeing our sons Nathan and Johnny hugging after the game in Hershey was a special moment as parents, and for their grandparents, aunts, uncles, and cousins that were there to see it.

2. We have described this team countless times with one word, *selfless*. That is the message we want to continue to tell you. Strive to be selfless. Put others before yourself and always put the team first. This team is the poster child of this. These boys never put themselves before the team. This 2018 season, and this whole journey, is a microcosm of life. There will be struggles and setbacks, but keep working hard, believing, persevering, and have trust in the friends that are around you. Some things are out of your control. But there are two things that you will *always* have control over: your work ethic and your attitude. A strong work ethic and a positive attitude will always lead to great things in your lives. We love you with all our hearts and we thank you for giving us these memories! Good luck! We will always be here for you!

Jeff and Louise Farelli:

1. One of my favorite memories of this group is when they went to camp freshman year. They were nervous, but not as nervous as the parents! You could see the boys' nervous energy as they prepared to leave and the parents frantically texting each other to be sure our "little boys" had everything they could possibly need. They seemed so little, and we were

sending them off, praying they would have a good experience and be OK with the older teammates. They would never admit that they were nervous, but you could see it in their faces as they boarded that bus. In my memory, they left as our little boys and grew so much during that week. They became a little more independent and confident in who they were as players and as young men. They learned to depend on, trust in, and to rely on each other as teammates, but more importantly, as friends.

2. I would describe this WA senior soccer class as a group of athletically gifted, competitive, and hardworking boys that were lucky enough to decide they all liked to play soccer together! Let's face it, any sport they would have focused on, they would've excelled at-they just have that kind of talent, work ethic and desire to win!

They have a wide array of personalities that we have been fortunate enough to witness grow into amazing young men! My hope is that they continue to be true to themselves and know they can achieve anything they set their mind too. Years from now, I hope they will remember this time of being one of the best soccer teams in the nation and achieving that title with some of their best friends beside them.

Mario and Debi Fiordilino:

1. There are so many incredible moments from this soccer season, especially with winning almost every game.

    Our favorite moments are playing Franklin Regional. We were so proud of the way they handled themselves after losing the WIPAL final at Highmark Stadium. They shed a few tears, picked themselves up and moved on, not letting that moment define them.

    Then having to face Franklin Regional again, without their goalie, in the semifinals, knowing the winner would move on to the state final. They took the field with confidence and determination and totally dominated for the win!

They are leaders-strong, confident, and driven young men that have developed a bond. Trust on the field and true friends off the field.

2. You can do anything as long as you have the passion, the drive, the focus, and the support!

—Mario Fiordilino

Always remember, true friends can go months, even years without talking but will always pick up right where they left off!

—Debi Fiordilino

Dave and Kristin Haines:

1. We often described Gabe's role as holding-mid as blue-collar. He never gets a lot of accolades. He works hard and plays well and appreciates the pats on the back and high fives from his coaches, teammates, and the fans. The run for states was challenging for Gabe personally, first, because he was injured, then because he took on the challenge of learning a brand-new position to replace Braden as keeper for the state semifinal game against our rivals, Franklin Regional. We are always proud of Gabe, but I never thought I could be more proud of Gabe as I was the night he stood in goal. I was wrong. Shortly after Gabe entered the state final game as a forward, Colin Wurst (brother of Braden our keeper and key player of the famed 2013 team) leaned forward and explained how Gabe's play was changing what was happening on the field. Winning states is by far the most special memory we'll ever have from high school. Knowing that Gabe played an important part in that victory makes it even sweeter.

2. I think WA will be hard-pressed to find a senior class that matches the caliber of our graduating boys. They all possess great character and willingness to put the team before individual goals. Their strong sense of brotherhood

was evident watching them play over the years. They are genuinely nice guys. We've been lucky to watch them grow from little boys to men. It was my honor to be the President of Boosters the boys' senior year. I loved being able to doing everything for them this year, from making the banners to packing the lunch bags.

Thank you for giving us the most special memories and taking us all the way to win the state championship. As parents, we never wanted this journey to end. Having it end with a state championship makes it hurt a little less. Remember what you accomplished on this team over the years and all the lessons you've learned through playing soccer. Nothing should ever stop you from achieving your dreams. You know it takes hard work. You face defeat. You keep going. And it's so worth it in the end. You'll always make us proud.

CHAPTER 21

Quotes from Our Team

Over the course of the 2018 season, our boys were interviewed many times in different newspapers and publications. We also did "man of the match" interviews after our games. Here are some quotes from our players and coaches over the season.

Kevin Amos after our state championship victory, talking about the neighborhood group of boys: "It's great that they win a state championship now. There's a lot of pickup games. A lot of the yards around here have nets in the back yards. I've used more grass seed than they do at Heinz Field."

Kevin Amos talking after our state championship victory about the M7 senior class when they first came in as freshmen: "They were all really small, and some of them were chubby and pudgy and everything else. How they've grown and just come to this, they've just put in the work and the dedication and they came out and proved it."

Antonio Fiordilino after our win against Hershey where he came in to play goalie after Braden was injured: "A few saves were definitely very unconventional saves, but I was just glad that I was able to get the job done today."

Fletcher Amos after our win over Franklin Regional in PIAA semifinals: "We wanted payback so bad, and we came in with some fire."

Evan Blunkosky after our 1-0 win over South Fayette early in the season: "I saw Jaxon over the ball, and I was able to make my run, but I fell. I saw the ball coming in, and I got up as quick as I possibly could, and I was able to put it in the back of the net."

Kevin Amos speaking about Nate Dragisich after a 4-1 win over Moon HS: "He's that player, we always talk about him buzzing during the game and getting going, and when he gets hungry and he's around the net, he'll do things just like that. You're usually looking for something special out of him when he gets inside the 18 and tonight, two goals inside the 18. He's dangerous."

Junior Caleb Miller talking to the *Tribune Review* about the defense after an 11-0 start to the season: "There is definitely a culture with the defense. We always try to keep a clean sheet. A 6-0 win is better than a 6-1 win. That's how we approach every game. Our first priority is to keep a clean sheet, but there is some pressure alleviated having an attack as good as ours."

Fletcher Amos talking to the *Tribune Review* about the team after an 11-0 start: "Last year was heartbreaking. We have high expectations this year and want to go on a run in states. It's been really fun this year. Our bench is really good, too. We have a lot of options. I think that gives us an advantage."

Kevin Amos talking about the team after an 11-0 start: "Our first priority always is to be unselfish. We probably have five guys that have seven or eight goals. That's key. If everything flows through one guy, we could be in trouble once playoffs start."

Caleb Miller speaking to the *Tribune Review* about set pieces and the team: "Every set piece or free kick, it's always fun to get up and get a chance to score. All our games are very entertaining for fans to watch. As a defender, it can drive you crazy with how much we attack. But, I love playing for this team."

Nate Dragisich speaking to the *Tribune Review* midway through the season: "We want to do something no other West A team has done, and that's win a state championship. This year, we have a lot of depth and a good starting lineup. That'll help us be able to compete for it."

Kevin Amos after our 2018 WPIAL semifinal victory over Mars HS: "That was two heavyweights out there tonight giving and taking their best shots all night."

Braden Wurst after kicking in the game winning PK in our victory over Mars HS: "I thought our fifth guy was coming up. I didn't realize we were going to our second five. I had an idea I might be in that range, but I still wasn't expecting it when he picked me."

Fletcher Amos talking about West A's offense to the *Tribune Review*: "It's really great scoring a lot of goals. Everyone wants to get on the scoresheet every game. Our team focuses on winning and getting the job done."

Gabe Haines after playing goalie in our state semifinal win over Franklin Regional: "A lot of pressure. I just tried to do my best and play for my team. It feels so good now. It feels so good."

Benny Farelli after a 2-0 win over Blackhawk while we played a man down for the last fifty-five minutes after a red card: "I think it mainly came down to the heart of our team and the fact that we persevered through the red card. We mainly outworked them today."

Nathan Dragisich after our state championship victory: "Today we played our best game. We played so well today and it shows on the scoreboard. We just knew that if we play our game, we can beat any team in the state."

Kevin Amos after our state championship victory: "I'm so proud of the boys. They worked really hard and we had a couple of setbacks in this section and had a loss to eventual champs Lower Dauphin last year, so they were really hungry and really wanted it and put up great numbers tonight."

Braden Wurst after our state championship victory: "I told my teammates before the semifinals, if you guys finish this game and you send us to the final, I promise I'll be back. My doctor told me it would be a miracle if I'd be back, but I worked so hard. It felt surreal. I'm just at a loss for words."

Nate Dragisich on his goal against Strath Haven to make it 2-0: "The free kick was called. I saw the goalie and the defenders arguing with the ref, and the net was wide open. I sprinted up to the ball, and I knew I had a chance to put it in. And I did."

Justin Shaytar on the strength of the West Allegheny defense: "It's mainly because we have been playing together for so many years. We have a lot of age in the back with two juniors and a senior, so we've been working together for a while, so we know each other and play well together."

Johnny Dragisich on playing with his older brother Nathan this year: "To be able to play with Nate is something I will never forget. He is such a huge role model for me, and he left some big shoes for me to fill."

Evan Blunkosky when asked about the header goals he scored after scoring two against Beaver Area HS: "Well, first off, I'd like to thank

Nate, as he supplies a lot of the balls into me. I just have confidence in the air, and I go in hard, and watch them go into the net."

Jaxon Ervin when asked about being a freshman starter playing on a team of senior and junior starters: "It's really fun. You can tell they've been playing with each other for years. And they treat me like a brother on the field. It's very intense, but we have each other's back."

Gavin Chappel talking about playing defense this season after playing midfield in his freshman and sophomore season: "I prefer playing up top as it's what I've been used to my whole life, but I'll do whatever it takes for the team to do what we need to do this season."

Freshman Will Douglas after scoring two goals in the first round of the state playoffs: "We played really good and got our confidence up, and we are ready to make a run at the state championship and win it."

Kevin Amos talking about Nate Dragisich to the *Tribune Review*: "He's a special player that comes around in high school every once in a while. He has a lot of natural talent and just works hard at it. He's a great teammate, great leader. He's someone who you can always count on to score a big goal when you really need it."

Braden Wurst after our playoff win against Mars: "Last year, we fell short to a section rival. This was our goal from the beginning of the year. We were fighting every practice, working hard, just to make it back to Highmark, and we had that mentality all season. We've tried to stick with one word and that's *unbeatable*."

Nate Dragisich after our state championship victory: "Getting it for the team and for the school, and never being a state champion before-it feels great. And doing it for the team, we're all friends, we all love this, we all wanted this, and we got it."

That completes the West Allegheny soccer journey! I truly love the families that I have spent the past fourteen years getting to know. We will all stay friends as our children move into the next chapter of life. I loved every minute of watching our boys become men. Boys, thank you for providing me and all of our families with ever lasting memories. I love you all. As soccer players and as young men, you are all *Unbeatable*!